LEADERSHIP
FOR STUDENTS

A PRACTICAL GUIDE
FOR AGES 8-18

FRANCES A. KARNES, PH.D.
SUZANNE M. BEAN, PH.D.

Copyright © 1995 by Frances A. Karnes and Suzanne M. Bean

ISBN 1-882664-12-4

Prufrock Press Post Office Box 8813
Waco, Texas 76714-8813
1-800-998-2208

Acknowledgements

This book is dedicated to members of our families. To Christopher, John, and Ray Karnes, who have been and will continue to be the reasons for all of my endeavors, I thank you for your understanding and patience.

—Frances A. Karnes

To my father, Ben K. Meriweather, who has helped me learn to understand, appreciate, and relate to people of all types—skills that are critical to understanding the concept of leadership and to becoming an effective leader.

—Suzanne M. Bean

Table of Contents

Preface

Everyone knows that there is a need for more effective leadership in all parts of society—schools, communities, religious groups, business and industry, government, and the arts. What is happening to the leadership in communities, states, and nations? Who are our great leaders? Because of the circumstances facing our nation and world, it is clear that more attention should be given to the development of leaders. Currently, there is a lack of support for the training of young leaders. It seems as if there is too little time or too little money to devote to training students in the area of leadership.

You have many characteristics that would allow you to benefit from development of your leadership potential. You have a high level of energy, the desire to be challenged, the courage to accomplish, and creative problem solving ability. Innovative approaches and purposeful direction are critically needed to help you realize your own leadership potential and to put your ideas into action!

Your commitment to developing leadership at an early age will certainly contribute to schools, communities, religious groups, and society as a whole. But more importantly, training for leadership will help you build a positive self-concept and experience personal fulfillment. Youth leadership development may be a productive approach for helping you avoid negative aspects of your environment and become involved with positive, meaningful experiences that will help you to develop into a responsible citizen.

You will enjoy reading the responses from others your age from across the country. You may want to think about how their responses are similar to or different from yours and your friends'. Each "Action" section following the responses provides many activities for you to complete. Some involve discussion for you and your friends, while others involve communication through reading and writing. For those of you who enjoy creative projects, there are suggestions in these areas as well. Other activities will guide you as you bring about positive changes in your school, community, or religious affiliation. All of the actions will help you to become involved as you develop your own leadership ability! Select the ones which will be most fun and helpful to you. There may be some activities which you might like to do immediately and others that may be completed later.

Leadership and Adults

Although this book has been written for you, the student, it will also be helpful to teachers, administrators, guidance counselors, librarians, parents, and community and religious leaders. Youth leadership training is an area that can and should be the responsibility of all of these groups of people.

For the teacher and school administrator, this book provides a national view of leadership. Teachers may include the activities in the curriculum within their classroom to encourage leadership potential in their students. Administrators will find the book helpful for planning school-wide leadership programs.

Other school personnel may use the book in a variety of ways. Many of the activities will have appeal to guidance counselors working in such areas as career education and personal growth and development. The book will also fill the void for school librarians who are frequently asked for books on leadership. Some of the activities may easily be undertaken in the school library or media center.

Currently, there are very few materials for parents wanting to develop and enhance the leadership potential of their child. These activities can easily be used in the home for discussion and family fun.

Community and religious leaders who work directly with students may incorporate the activities into the framework of their organizations, too. Scouting leaders, members of chambers of commerce, adult civic groups, religious personnel, and others who work with youth may use the book as a guide for understanding students' perceptions of leadership and for developing youth leadership experiences.

We hope that you will share this book with these and other adults who are interested in developing the leadership potential of youth.

What's Ahead for You

Interactions with students through leadership training programs led us to the realization of the need for a more systematic process for leadership training. We initiated a survey to find student perceptions of leadership, and a pool of questions relating to leadership was identified by us and others. We then selected 19 questions for the survey. Student responses to the questions in the "Ideas" sections of the book were received from across the nation. We conducted conference presentations on youth leadership development, and participants in these sessions often volunteered to have their students respond to the survey items. A variety of journals, newsletters, and other publications included notices about the study, and many contacts were made through the publications. We invited other educators to participate.

After all responses had been collected, a panel of reviewers separately analyzed the responses and selected those they thought would most represent those students. We then collected the selections offered by the panel reviewers and made the final determination of the responses to be included in the book.

We designed activities relating to each of the survey items ranging from very simple to complex. Students then rated the ideas and actions for each chapter in the book. Their input was valuable in making the "Actions" sections more interesting for students. We planned activities to provide a variety of types of experiences from which to choose.

In the "Introduction to Leadership" you will find information on myths or misconceptions people have about leadership and how they relate to many obstacles people face when becoming leaders. You will also discover new information on the moral and ethical dimensions of leadership. Finally, you will gain strategies and tips for time management which will help you as you manage your day-to-day schedule with school work, extracurricular and community activities, family, and friends. That's quite a lot to juggle as you work toward becoming a more effective leader, but you can do it!

Following the "Introduction to Leadership," there are seven chapters. The first chapter, Defining Leadership, focuses on the definitions, characteristics, and the positive and negative aspects of leadership. Chapter 2, Assessing Yourself as a Leader, stresses ways of knowing if you are a leader, attitudes toward being one, and the self-perceived strongest and weakest areas of leadership. Chapter 3, Opportunities for Leadership, indicates those experiences for leadership which are available in schools, communities, and religious affiliations. In Chapter 4, Training for Leadership, opportunities for leadership education are explored in these three environments. Chapter 5, Influence and Encouragement from Others, sets forth ideas on those who assist in the development of leadership potential. In Chapter 6, Great Leaders, many ideas and activities are given to develop the students' concepts of those who may serve as role models in leadership. In the last chapter, Chapter 7, Advice to Others, the students surveyed offer advice to other students who would like to become leaders.

Within each chapter of the book you will find ideas and actions for each question relating to leadership. The beginning of each chapter features a brief summary of the students' responses to each question. The "Ideas" sections contain the students' responses from the questions on leadership. The responses range from brief to elaborate. Immediately following the "Ideas" section is the "Actions" segment, which includes a variety of activities to enhance your knowledge of and skills in leadership. Some of the activities will be more appealing to those of you who are younger or have less previous interest or knowledge of leadership, while others will be more meaningful to those of you with some background and experience. All activities have been designed for you to complete in a self-directed manner. Products, which may be written or visual, have been suggested as outcomes of your work in leadership. You may substitute other products which may be more in line with your abilities, interests, or resources.

In the "Individual and Group Leadership Accomplishments" section, you will find stories of leadership in the community and in the school. The stories are provided by individuals and groups of young people. They are inspiring and amazing, and you'll enjoy reading of these students' many accomplishments. The "Leadership Action Journal" section in the second half of the book provides reproducible pages for you to record your thoughts and actions. The activities found in the "Action" sections of the book marked with the "Action Journal" symbol are in the "Leadership Action Journal." The next section, "Leadership Action Forms," includes general forms for you to use as you engage in your actions. You may find these forms particularly helpful in writing letters, making contacts, conducting and analyzing surveys, or developing plans for leadership, among other things. Next, you will find a list of resources. You may contact these places for more information on leadership opportunities. The last section, "Get In Touch," invites you to share your ideas with us.

Thanks to All

We are indebted to the many students and adults who gave freely of their time, effort, and expertise during the several phases of this work. We are especially grateful to several professional associates in the field of leadership research, development, and training who assisted with the selection, conceptualization, and wording of the questions included in the final form of the survey instrument. Their critical review of early drafts and the changes, deletions, and additions suggested were invaluable in the process of structuring items which would elicit useful responses.

An expression of appreciation is extended to the editors and publishers of the several journals, magazines, and newsletters in which announcements of the survey appeared. References in their publications prompted many teachers, other school personnel, and parents to request copies of the survey instrument and to express interest in participating in the study.

We owe special thanks to school administrators and to the teachers who provided their students with an opportunity to participate. The survey responses submitted by students were clearly indicative of a genuine interest in leadership on their part. We are not only grateful to those students but inspired by them as well. A special appreciation is felt for the individuals and groups of students and their teachers who provided the excellent stories of leadership in schools and communities.

Jim Delisle gave generously of his advice and counsel during the initial stages of this undertaking, and for this we are exceedingly grateful. We were assisted in another important way toward the end of the project by several professional colleagues and by students who participated in the selection of specific responses and activities to be included in the book. For this valuable contribution we wish to express our sincere gratitude.

The faculty, staff, and administration at our respective institutions continue to encourage us, and for that support we are grateful. To those who have given technical support in the preparation of the manuscript, including Sherry Honsinger, we extend a special thanks.

Thanks to Linda Meylan, who was thorough and precise in ensuring that the manuscript met technical and professional standards. Also, to Tracy Riley and Janet Hugo who served as readers of the manuscript, we appreciate your time and expertise.

To our families we give special recognition and words of appreciation. To Ray and Mark, who serve as leadership role models to us, our special thanks for your patience, devotion, and support. To our children, Christopher, John, and Meriweather, words cannot express our love and happiness with you.

Introduction to Leadership

Shortly after birth we begin on a life-long journey of learning to interact with other people—first family members and later friends, schoolmates, peers, colleagues, and business associates. As preschool children, we learn to negotiate the use of playground equipment and make compromises over toys. As school-aged students, we test our own potential at forming friendships and influencing others. Later in school, church, and the community, we join or form groups, clubs, and organizations, and we begin to learn the art of weaving relationships as we work with others toward common goals. This is the foundation from which leadership develops.

As we experience the processes of leadership, it is hoped that many characteristics will form—self-confidence, initiative, communication skills, energy, and responsibility—to name a few. Yet many young people often fail to develop as leaders. Why does human potential toward leadership remain underdeveloped? What are the forces that work against the development of effective leaders? Why is strong leadership ability sometimes channeled in negative, unethical directions?

Misconceptions of Leadership

Many confusing messages about leadership are relayed to young people throughout society—in homes, schools, and communities across the nation. Often misconceptions are formed in our minds based on these messages we receive. For example, if all the leaders in your school and community are male, you might assume, "Boys make better leaders than girls." This is a misconception that you have formed from the messages you have received from your environment.

Examine the listing of "Leadership Misconceptions and Related Facts," and discuss them with your friends, classmates, etc. Where do these misconceptions begin, and how are they perpetuated? How can you help to dispel these misconceptions?

Leadership Misconceptions and Related Facts

Boys make better leaders than girls.	Individual differences in leadership *styles* contribute more to effective leadership than do gender differences.
	Females are becoming more actively involved in leadership roles in politics, business, the arts, education, and other areas.

Think about Joan of Arc, Indira Gandhi, and Eleanor Roosevelt.

First-born children make better leaders than their later-born siblings.	The opportunities for leadership development any child experiences have more to do with his or her abilities to lead than his or her position in the family.

Think about John Kennedy and Babe Zaharius.

One must be elected or appointed to be a leader.	Many non-elected or non-appointed people throughout history are now recognized as outstanding leaders in their respective fields.
	Many people have earned their leadership positions through hard work— not elections.
	There are people in your own school and community who have not been elected or appointed to leadership but who are considered leaders or "take charge" people by their friends.

Think about Mother Teresa and Benjamin Franklin.

You have to be popular to be an effective leader.	Many people throughout history have proved themselves as outstanding leaders, yet they were not popular when they began their journey as a leader.
	Leadership is often earned through actions, not popularity.
	Sometimes people in student government organizations or school clubs may be elected on popularity rather than leadership ability. They often don't get the job done either!

Think about Harry Truman and Frances Perkins.

You can't be a leader if you live in a small, rural community.	In small schools and communities, young people have greater opportunities to participate and lead in multiple activities.
	Many of our great leaders of today spent most of their formative years in small, rural communities and schools.

Think about Rosa Parks, Jimmy Carter, and Bill Clinton.

Children and young people can't really lead.	Although most of the research on leadership has looked at adult leaders, young leaders have made a significant impact on the world.
	People develop skills in leadership at a very early age.

Think about the students in the leadership stories in this book.

| Only people from the majority culture can be effective leaders. | People from all races and cultural backgrounds have leadership potential. People from diverse cultures may express their leadership abilities differently, but one's race or culture does not determine the level of leadership ability he or she has. |

Think about Barbara Jordan, Cesar Chavez, and Oprah Winfrey.

| You have to be rich to be a good leader. | One's level of wealth has nothing to do with leadership ability. Many people from poor backgrounds are highly effective leaders. |

Think about Martin Luther King, Jr., Jim Thorpe, and Mary McLeod Bethune.

| You have to be outgoing to be an effective leader. | There are effective leaders who are reserved. Some may work behind the scenes, while others may lead with a more quiet style. |

Think about Rachel Carson and Mohandas K. Gandhi.

| You have to make straight A's in school to be a good leader. | Superior academic ability or intelligence is not an absolute requirement for leadership. A person who works hard in school to be the best that he or she can be usually has the perseverance to be a good leader. |

Think about Winston Churchill, Ann Bancroft, and Nelson Rockefeller.

| Only schools offer opportunities for leadership. | Schools should offer real experiences for leadership through clubs and organizations, but opportunities for leadership may also be found in families, neighborhoods, communities, and in religious affiliations. |

Think about opportunities for leadership in your own community.

Creative Problem Solving
Fuzzy Situations Regarding Leadership Misconceptions

Christina is a 10th grade student at Hudson High School who is interested in developing her leadership potential. She is a member of several clubs but has never been elected as an officer. Christina is somewhat shy and has a few very close friends; however, she would not be considered one of the most popular students in school. She is particularly interested in the student government. Most of the members of the Hudson High Student Government Association are male. In what ways might Christina develop her leadership potential?

Bob is a sixth grade student who comes from an economically disadvantaged family background and attends school in a small community. The total population of the town is 2,462. Bob works hard in school and gets along well with young people and adults. He is interested in many areas including wildlife, the environment, drawing, and math. His greatest strength is his sense of humor. Bob wants to develop his leadership skills. In what ways might he accomplish this?

Obstacles to Becoming a Leader

Sometimes your own "personal forces" and mistakes in life can interfere with your growth as a leader. For example, when you attempt a goal that is too far out of your reach at that time, you often fail to achieve the goal, which may result in a loss of self-confidence. A lack of self-confidence is an obstacle to leadership development. These and other obstacles can be overcome through recognition of them and consistent efforts to improve in these areas.

Look at the "Obstacles to Becoming a Leader and Alternatives Toward Leadership Development." What are other obstacles you have experienced in your pursuit of leadership potential? What alternatives have you found successful in overcoming these obstacles?

···

Obstacles to Becoming a Leader
and Alternatives Toward Leadership Development

Lack of self-confidence

Engage yourself in activities that help build your confidence, and surround yourself with people who encourage your abilities.

Negative Attitudes

- "There's nothing I can do about it"
- "That's just the way I am"
- "I'm sure they won't allow us to do that"

Work on developing an "I Can" attitude or at least an "I'll Try" attitude. Effective leaders have positive attitudes!

Extreme Shyness

Try getting involved in activities that include a few other people rather than large groups. This may help you to become more comfortable with others, and you can gradually work up to larger groups.

Lack of ability to listen to others

Learn to keep your mouth closed more and your ears and mind open to the ideas of others.

Not setting priorities

Choose the activities that are most important to you. One who tries to do everything may find that he or she is not really effective at anything!

Not setting goals

When priorities have been determined, set your goals toward completion of activities or projects. How will you know where you are going if you don't choose a path to follow?

Wanting and trying to do it all yourself

Some people strive for power and recognition rather than real leadership. You must realize that an effective leader is also a team player! Work hard to make sure all members of the group are actively involved and are recognized for their contributions.

···

Lack of perseverance

Some people start many projects but have a difficult time finishing them. This usually means they lack "stick-to-it-ness." Effective leaders must not give up on projects they start no matter how difficult or time consuming they may be!

Time Management

One major obstacle to becoming a leader is a lack of time management. Effective leaders must be in charge of their own time and must organize and work around priorities. Managing your time effectively determines the quality of your leadership.

Many young people aspiring toward leadership find this obstacle to be a most difficult one to master. It is often very easy to "put things off" until the last minute or to choose only the fun or easy activities to do, but procrastination is a significant hindrance to productive leadership. The results of procrastination can be restricting in leadership development and in personal growth as well.

Analyze the "Time Management Matrix" and assess your own ability in this area. What are the activities that keep you from being as productive as you could be? How do you spend most of your free time? How can you make better use of your time?

Time Management Matrix

Procrastinators ...

- Are unorganized
- Welcome and accept interruptions
- Work on insignificant activities
- Day dream
- Try to take on too many activities
- Talk rather than do
- Don't make choices, or choose fun activities only
- Put things off until the deadline arrives
- Are reactive

Effective Time Managers ...

- Set priorities
- Eliminate unnecessary activities
- Set goals
- Get organized
- Use calendars or appointment books
- Make and use lists
- Engage in daily planning
- Make choices
- Are proactive
- Delegate tasks to others

Results

Procrastinators ...

- Have stress
- Burn out
- Feel out of control
- Break promises
- Suffer a decrease in self-esteem
- Lose respect for others
- Are irresponsible
- Depend on others

Effective Time Managers ...

- Have discipline
- Have control
- Have balance
- Are productive
- Are self-reliant
- Increase their self-esteem
- Have respect for others
- Are responsible
- Obtain leadership

Moral and Ethical Dimensions of Leadership

Leadership with ethics leads to service to humanity. To what does leadership without ethics lead? Can someone be an effective leader without acceptable moral or ethical standards? How about Hitler? Sometimes leadership ability is channeled in a negative direction resulting in manipulation and corruption. For example, the gang leader may have strong leadership ability, but sometimes uses this ability in a destructive way. Too often we focus on the mechanics of leadership, and we neglect one of the most important dimensions— the heart of leadership—morality and ethics.

Examine the "Moral and Ethical Dimensions of Leadership." Does power corrupt? How are acceptable moral and ethical standards set? What determines a morally mature leader? Are there leaders who have had unethical causes, but moral actions? Are there leaders who have had moral causes, but unethical actions? What is your plan for your own growth toward becoming an ethical leader?

Moral and Ethical Dimensions of Leadership

Leaders Who Lack Morality or Ethics May ...

- be cruel to their own group members
- treat followers well, but encourage them to do evil things to others
- use followers' weaknesses like fear, paranoia, hate, bigotry, or desire for revenge
- manipulate group members
- diminish their followers, making them dependent and child-like
- believe that the end justifies the means
- distort reality and use propaganda
- set group members against one another
- use intimidation, threats, bribery, and coercion to motivate
- be self-serving and egocentric
- lack sensitivity to others' needs
- be dominated by group values or peer pressure
- lack their own set of values, standards, and ideals

Morally Acceptable Leaders ...

- serve the common good and at the same time pay attention to individual interests
- transmit a sense of mission
- encourage followers to go beyond their own self interests
- promote harmony
- demonstrate integrity
- are compassionate and sensitive to the needs of others
- are authentic
- resolve conflicts fairly
- share in the leadership tasks
- work toward releasing human possibilities
- foster individual initiative, but expect a certain amount of initiative to be expended on shared purposes
- are tolerant and hold mutual respect for others
- enrich commitment to freedom, justice, equality of opportunity, and dignity and worth of the individual

Examples from History of Leaders who Lack Morality or Ethics	Examples from History of Morally Acceptable Leaders
Adolf Hitler	Rachel Carson
Idi Amin	Mohandas Ghandi
Joseph Stalin	Martin Luther King, Jr.
Ayatollah Khomeni	George Washington
James Jones	Indira Gandhi

Final Thoughts

When we really analyze the concept of leadership, we find that there are many new dimensions to be explored—misconceptions and how they can be disproven, obstacles and how they can be overcome, and moral and ethical leadership and why and how it should be developed. These and other such facts as related to leadership help to provide the ingredients for the preparation of young leaders. If young people do not seriously prepare for positions of leadership, our schools, communities, nation, and world will suffer! Society's call for more effective leaders may be answered by one essential element—young people who are dedicated to preparing themselves for lives of leadership and service.

Chapter 1
Defining Leadership

What is leadership?

Our survey said that although some of the elementary age students refer to leadership as power, authority, and control, the majority of students defined leadership in positive terms. The responses reflect a wide range of characteristics and behaviors of leadership. In general, the older students identified leadership as a multidimensional concept.

Ideas

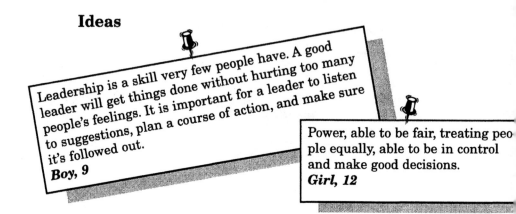

Leadership is a skill very few people have. A good leader will get things done without hurting too many people's feelings. It is important for a leader to listen to suggestions, plan a course of action, and make sure it's followed out.
Boy, 9

Power, able to be fair, treating people equally, able to be in control and make good decisions.
Girl, 12

Leadership is guiding and showing the way for other people, to get people to cooperate and do things together, to lead a group, to make them cooperate with one another.
Boy, 11

The ability to be looked upon as a role model.
Girl, 12

Being able to stand up for what you believe in, having authority over most people, making new ideas, not following old ones.
Boy, 12

The ability to take on responsibility and work with a group of people in an orderly, productive way.
Girl, 13

Leadership is being able to guide people in times of crisis or in other situations. It is being able to make good decisions and having a great sense of responsibility. Also, it is being helpful when possible.
Girl, 13

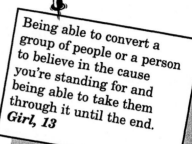

Being able to convert a group of people or a person to believe in the cause you're standing for and being able to take them through it until the end.
Girl, 13

Leadership is the ability to have influence over the actions and/or opinions of a group.
Girl, 13

Leadership is the ability to lead people or represent them. It all starts with responsibility. Your actions don't only affect you, but everyone you represent.
Boy, 13

Leadership is the ability to work with your peers effectively and to guide and cooperate with them. It is to be one's own self, trying not to be a replica of another.
Girl, 14

Leadership is a form of responsibility, you must be organized and self-confident to be a leader. You must also be able to listen to whomever you are leading.
Boy, 14

Leadership is the ability to take authority and responsibility and use it wisely in order to bring progress and success to a particular group, institution, club, family, etc.
Boy, 15

Leadership is the ability to take on the challenge of improving the school, attitude of peers, and one's own inclination to be a leader. A leader is a representative. His or her job is to best represent the people that elected him or her as their voice.
Girl, 17

The ability to take charge and direct groups toward a goal.
Girl, 15

It's a willingness to take command, not to domineer over others, but to bring people together for one purpose. To keep things focused and make sure the job gets done.
Girl, 17

The ability to motivate others for a positive action.
Boy, 16

Leadership is responsibility, the willingness to help others, and the ability to make unpopular decisions for the good of the purpose.
Girl, 17

Being able to lead, head, or guide a group or groups of people to successful accomplishments.
Boy, 17

Leadership, in actuality, is servitude. It is not how well you boss people around or how charismatic you are. Leadership is how well you serve, whether it be your class, or a country. The best leaders make the best servants.
Boy, 16

Actions

 # Think About It

Which one of the definitions of leadership do you like best? Why?

What is your definition of leadership?

Survey your friends to get their ideas on definitions of leadership.

What is the definition of leadership in the dictionary? Compare it to those given by students from across the U.S. Compare it to your definition of leadership.

Think of three famous leaders (political, religious, social, etc.). What do you think their definitions of leadership would be? How would their definitions be alike? How would they be different?

How do you think leadership will be different when you are an adult or in 20 years? How will you prepare for this?

Choose three leaders from different areas and research them. Perhaps you will choose a religious, political, social, or business leader, or one in the arts, humanities, or sports. Which one appeals most to you? Analyze his or her responsibilities.

Name students you know who fit your definition of leadership. What qualities of theirs would you like to develop or enhance for yourself?

 # Talk About It

Think of your three favorite movies. Which ones have an element of "leadership" within the story? Discuss this with your friends.

 # Write About It

Write a short story, poem, essay, or song based on your definition of leadership.

What will be the definition of leadership in the next century?

Write a story on leadership for your school newspaper.

Do It

What information does the encyclopedia have on leadership? Do you agree or disagree with the information? If you disagree with the information, write what you think should be included in an encyclopedia section on leadership and send it to the publisher.

Make a poster of what leadership is or means to you. Ask your principal to hang it in your school. Ask if your principal or art teacher would like to sponsor a school art contest.

 Make a bumper sticker of leadership. Ask a club in your school or community to have it made and sold to raise funds for a leadership training program for youth.

Some people think of leadership as being the same as popularity. What do you think? Conduct a debate or panel discussion with some of your friends or classmates on this topic.

Ask five leaders in your school to talk to your class or club about what they think leadership is and compare their responses.

 Look at leadership in a new way. What is the color of leadership? What is the smell of leadership? If you could touch leadership, how would it feel? Use your responses to these questions to make a sculpture or some other visual display of leadership and show it in your school or community.

How is leadership connected to other disciplines and components of society? Using the web on page 125 as a guide, create a model or a diagram of connections with leadership.

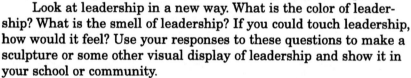

What are the most important characteristics for being a leader?

Our survey showed that students offered a wide variety of characteristics of a leader; however, several characteristics emerged as the most frequently cited. Those characteristics were communication, responsibility, self-confidence, intelligence, and decision making skills. Other responses not cited frequently, but important to leadership, were perception, control of emotions, a strong sense of morality, and the ability to take a risk. The responses indicated that the students were well–informed of the characteristics of leaders.

Ideas

Good communication, manages time well, organized, good listener, patience, they don't quit.
Boy, 10

To be truthful, understanding, determined, nice, and able to hold responsibility.
Girl, 9

The most important characteristic for being a leader is that he or she believes in what he or she does, he or she is able to talk out in front of people, make accurate decisions, and listen to everybody's ideas and try to put them all into one.
Boy, 10

High-spirited, dedicated, responsible, hard working, friendly, have pride in self.
Girl, 13

I think the most important characteristics for being a leader are responsibility, listening to all sides, confidence in yourself.
Girl, 11

The leader must not think of him or herself as the only boss. He or she must listen to all the ideas and make the right choice for the group. He or she must always consider the group's feelings.
Boy, 13

To be a good leader, you have to be a good communicator.
Boy, 12

rsistence, politeness, intelli-
nce, good sense of right and
rong, reasoning.
.oy, 10

To show responsibility and be a good role model to other students.
Girl, 12

Charisma, patience, self-confidence, and respect, responsibility, dependability.
Girl, 14

Unprejudiced, understanding, fair, honest, diplomatic, open-minded.
Girl, 14

Charisma, calmness, strength, wisdom, intelligence, ambition, patience.
Boy, 14

Must stand for what they think is right, they still must be able to listen and negotiate with other leaders, must be considerate to the needs of the groups they are leading.
Girl, 14

Charisma, intelligence, willingness to compromise, confidence, ability to speak or express yourself, assertiveness.
Boy, 16

Confidence, determination, foresight, risk–taker, belief in others, idealism, realism, creativeness.
Girl, 17

I think the most important characteristic is the ability to listen and communicate. A leader must be able to hear other's ideas and complaints and follow through with them. He or she has to communicate with all types of people, and be able to get points across to them.
Girl, 17

Some important characteristics of a leader are mental stability, ability to properly handle various crises, and a strong sense of morality and thought of the people, not one's self.
Boy, 16

You must be outgoing, responsible, willing to work hard, easy to get along with, tactful but not forceful, and full of enthusiasm.
Girl, 15

A leader has to be flexible, able to adapt in any situation, able to make good decisions, and give credit to others and take criticism.
Boy, 17

The most important characteristics of a leader are having the ability to creatively and logically approach a problem and to effectively communicate ideas and methods of accomplishment of the tasks.
Girl, 17

Brave, not shy.
Boy, 15

One must be able to lead in the right direction, one must be eager to learn and listen to others, one must be humble, one who can be respected by others, one who others look highly upon, one must be responsible, able to take on responsibility, one must be able to overcome obstacles.
Girl, 17

Listening to others, quick, positive actions, high goals, optimism/realism, flexibility, able to roll with the punches, stubbornness when working toward a goal.
Girl, 18

Actions

💡 Think About It

Are there other important characteristics of leadership which have not been mentioned?

List characteristics of leadership which you think are important and rate yourself on these characteristics.

How will you develop your weak areas?

Think of one female and one male leader. List and compare the leadership characteristics of each. What are the similarities? The differences?

Read About It

Read several articles or books on great leaders and make a chart with their characteristics of leadership.

 # Write About It

After reading about leaders, write a short essay about the characteristics of your favorite leaders. List negative characteristics of each leader from the above stories. List positive characteristics of each leader from the above stories.

Which characteristics do you have?

Try to name a characteristic of leadership for each letter of the alphabet.

 Brainstorm characteristics of leadership. Group your responses according to those characteristics that you believe people are born with and those characteristics that people must learn.

 # Do It

Conduct a survey by asking your friends what they believe to be the most important characteristics for being a good leader. Make a chart showing the results and post it in your classroom or in the hall in your school. Be sure to get permission.

Investigate the new information that has been written on the differences in male and female leadership characteristics. Create a play or short drama enacting the male and female styles of leadership. Make projections as to how you think the shift in leadership characteristics and styles will change society. Debate this topic with friends.

Create a cartoon character who has all of the characteristics of leadership that you think are important. Write a story about that character and his or her ideas about leadership. Share the story with younger students.

What are the positive aspects of being a leader?

The nature of the students' responses to this question indicates that the majority of students have experienced a leadership position. The most frequently cited positive aspects of being a leader were helping others, the sense of being needed, belonging to a group, the feeling of accomplishment upon achievement of a goal, self growth and understanding, and gaining the respect of others.

Ideas

You feel needed, you have a sense of belonging in the world. It's great.
Girl, 11

Self-fulfillment, responsibility, and respect.
Boy, 12

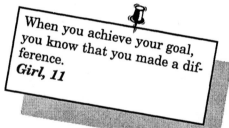

When you achieve your goal, you know that you made a difference.
Girl, 11

You get a chance to make decisions and be part of an organization.
Girl, 12

You have the feeling of pride and responsibility.
Boy, 9

You can see how creative you can be with your group.
Girl, 13

As a leader, I feel that I can meet people and make more close friends. I can learn more about other people and myself. I have a better chance of helping people and getting other people involved in projects. I get a good feeling about a job well done. I also learn to accept criticism.
Boy, 12

You can change things that don't appeal to you. You are an important part of your community.
Girl, 13

You can make things better for other people.
Boy, 13

Feeling of accomplishment, having the respect of a group, being able to get people to work together.
Girl, 13

As a leader, you can learn to think for yourself and become responsible for your actions as they will affect you and your peers.
Girl, 14

It gives you a feeling of accomplishment. It makes you feel like there is nothing you can't do if you try hard enough.
Girl, 15

Preparation to succeed in life.
Boy, 16

A leader is gratified by helping a group and the results of what they accomplish.
Girl, 16

You gain a feeling of achievement and worthiness.
Girl, 17

You develop a good self-esteem and you learn a lot about other people and yourself. It makes you a better person.
Girl, 16

The positive aspects are the respect others have for me and the sense of accomplishment attained when a project under my leadership is completed in an effective manner.
Girl, 17

Actions

 # Think About It

Review the responses given by the students and select the ones which would be like yours and state why.

How do you think Abraham Lincoln, Martin L. King Jr., Florence Nightengale, or Eleanor Roosevelt would respond to the same question?

 # Write About It

Make your own list of the positive aspects of being a leader.

 # Talk About It

Interview your school principal and counselor and ask them about the positive aspects of their leadership positions and their ideas on effective leadership. Design a way to let students know the results.

 # Do It

Think of leaders in the categories of religion, arts, science, government, politics, etc. Contact one in each category and ask for a statement from each on the positive aspects of being a leader from their perspective. Develop a display to share with your friends and other students.

Write a skit for younger children that shows the positive things about being a leader. Present the skit to a group of younger children in your school, community, or religious affiliation.

Examine the changes that have occurred in leadership since the beginning of time. Design a docudrama of this historical perspective of leadership and focus on the positive aspects of being a leader in today's society.

Design a poster of leaders and what each would say are the positive aspects of leadership.

Interview student leaders in your school, community, or religious affiliation and ask them what they think the positive aspects of being a leader are. Compare the responses that were given. Do those leaders have the same ideas about positive aspects of leadership? How are their responses different according to their positions of leadership? Compare your responses to those given. Make a poster with the results and post it in your school or community facility. Be sure to ask permission.

What are the negative aspects of being a leader?

Our survey revealed that the majority of responses have to do with the way other people may respond to someone in a leadership position. Specific reactions from others that the students identified as negative were hate, jealousy, loss of faith, criticism, blame, and rejection. Other negative aspects of leadership cited were stress, pressure, the lack of privacy, the possibility of making a mistake, and the amount of time required of someone in a leadership position.

Ideas

Betrayal.
Boy, 11

The negative aspects of being a leader are making the wrong decision, people might get hurt, and everyone ignoring you.
Boy, 10

The negative aspects are that if one of your suggestions or solutions that you tried bombed out and everyone was disappointed, they might lose faith in you.
Girl, 10

When you are wrong, you carry the blame. Someone is always criticizing you.
Boy, 10

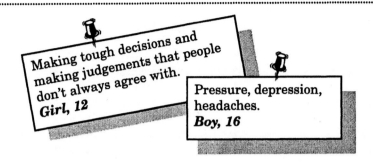

Making tough decisions and making judgements that people don't always agree with.
Girl, 12

Pressure, depression, headaches.
Boy, 16

Time and unresponsive people.
Boy, 12

A negative aspect is that if your success goes to your head and you become bossy, your followers will turn against you.
Girl, 12

If you make a mistake, you could affect a lot of people because they were depending on you.
Girl, 12

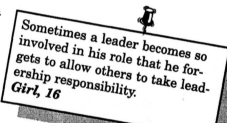

Sometimes a leader becomes so involved in his role that he forgets to allow others to take leadership responsibility.
Girl, 16

Sometimes you have to do things that you don't like.
Girl, 13

It gets hard at times, you get looked upon differently, like you're expected to be perfect.
Girl, 13

Stress, time–consuming, people could dislike you because of the decisions you make.
Girl, 14

Pressure to always excel.
Girl, 15

Feeling bad when you did not help someone enough.
Girl, 17

You lose sense of your needs or stress yourself to do too much. You have no private life.
Girl, 17

Loss of personal time. Many times I will be pressed into leadership roles even when I don't really wish to participate. It greatly imposes on my personal time.
Girl, 17

Actions

 # Think About It

What do you believe to be or have you experienced as the negative aspects of leadership?

What would you say to a friend who only thinks of the negative side of leadership?

As a leader, how would you deal with criticism, jealousy, unrealistic expectations, loss of personal time, and pressures?

How would you handle a situation in which you, as the leader, were unjustly blamed for the failure of a project?

Imagine that you are an important leader of a big group. What would you like to say to your followers that may prevent negative attitudes?

 # Read About It

Read about the life of a famous leader and list what he or she might consider to be the negative aspects of leadership.

 # Do It

Organize a debate on the positive and negative sides of leadership.

How would you convince other young people that developing leadership skills can be very positive for them personally and professionally? Develop a plan of action for this goal and put it to work.

As a leader, how would you deal with or overcome the part of leadership which you think is negative? List the negative aspects of leadership and ways you could turn them into positives.

Interview leaders in your school or community and ask what they think the negative aspects are and how they deal with them.

Prepare a speech or a paper on topics such as: "The Positive and Negative Aspects of Leadership," "How to Turn the Negatives of Leadership into Positives," etc. Present it to an appropriate group of students.

Chapter 2
Assessing Yourself as a Leader

How do you know you are a leader?

Our survey found that all of the students responding to this question do believe that they are leaders. Some students stated that they know they are leaders because of the way others treat them with respect and as role models. Other students cited personal qualities as indicators of their ability to lead such as comfort in leadership positions, being a trend–setter, persuasiveness, the ability to withstand peer pressure, and the ability to take charge.

Ideas

When you are a leader, you know it because people trust you and look up to you.
Boy, 11

I like to help other people, I can handle my responsibilities, and I like to plan activities.
Girl, 12

I never quit. I go to the end.
Boy, 10

By being able to solve problems easily.
Girl, 9

I know how to cooperate with others, and I know how to get things done.
Girl, 10

I am mostly sure of myself. People like me and sometimes follow my advice. They choose me for the leader in some games.
Girl, 10

I am not afraid of what they are going to say about my ideas.
Girl, 11

I know I am a leader because I find myself helping with special activities and participating in everyday meetings with people who I know are leaders.
Girl, 13

I make things happen in groups.
Boy, 12

If you have willpower and strong motivation to set and reach personal goals, then most likely you have the qualities that leadership requires.
Boy, 15

I am a leader because I am not only interested in my own ideas and actions when I am in a group, but also care about voicing or representing someone else's opinion who may be less willing to communicate. If I feel that things are not getting done, I can easily take it upon myself to start the action.
Girl, 16

People look up to you and depend on you to support and help them, people use you as an example.
Boy, 14

I'm often the first in school to try something and people generally follow, because they trust me. I always have an opinion on a subject, yet don't let that get in the way of seeing the other side of the subject.
Girl, 14

You can make people see your ideas and people will follow you.
Girl, 13

By the outcomes of my actions, I help people get involved and work to improve some things.
Girl, 17

I know that I am a leader because people will come up to me and ask me questions regarding the class. I feel that I am able to take charge of things if I have to, I am able to accomplish any tasks I set out to do.
Girl, 17

Respect of peers, adults, teachers, and parents, looked up to, opinion held in high regard.
Girl, 18

Actions

Think About It

Which responses of the students would be similar to yours?
Why is it important for a good leader to also be a good follower?
Which ones are different? Why?
What are the characteristics of a good follower?
How would you rate yourself on these characteristics?

Write About It

Prepare a speech about your abilities as a leader and use it as a campaign speech as if you want to run for office.

List the ways that you have been a leader either formally or informally.

List the ways that you have been a leader in your school, community, or religious affiliation. Circle the leadership roles which you have enjoyed the most. Write the reasons why you liked the roles that you circled and the reasons why you didn't like the others.

Keep a log or a diary for a year and record all the ways you were a leader.

Make a list of all the extracurricular activities in which you are involved (include clubs, organizations, hobbies, etc.). Analyze your role in these groups. Do you usually take charge of activities? Do you usually wait for someone else to tell you what to do?

How do you see yourself as a leader in the future? Write a scenario of your life as a leader 15 years from now. Write a description of the types of leadership experience you will have, the ideas to be conveyed, the leadership style used, and the feelings of leadership.

 Do It

Draw a picture or make a collage of how you see yourself as a leader during the coming year.

Make a list of other extracurricular activities in which you would like to be involved. Come up with strategies for getting involved in these activities.

Think of one or two people whom you consider to be leaders. Make a list of characteristics or behaviors that these people possess. Rate yourself 1–5 on each of these items (1 being low and 5 being high).

Initiate a "Leader of the Month" program in your school or community. This would give recognition to the young person who has shown leadership ability over the given time period. Ask for support for this proposal from the local chamber of commerce, community groups, adult leaders, etc.

What is your attitude toward being a leader?

Our survey said that students regarded leadership with pride, honor, and a degree of seriousness. They also stated that being a leader is fun, challenging, and very rewarding. Some students felt that leadership should be a shared responsibility because too much leadership from one person can result in a negative situation.

Ideas

I like the responsibility.
Boy, 10

My attitude toward being a leader is a good attitude. I know that if I am not in the spotlight and someone else is, I should treat them the way I want to be treated. If I give them respect, they will usually give me respect back.
Girl, 10

I feel that with the title comes much responsibility, and I feel I must live up to other's expectations.
Boy, 16

I think that being a good leader is very important to your future.
Girl, 10

I feel that if someone is able to withstand the challenge and responsibility, then they should go for it. But if they are only doing it for themselves and not to help others, then they should just forget it.
Girl, 13

My attitude is serious if I really want to be a good leader. I like being a leader, but I don't let it go to my head.
Girl, 13

By being a leader, you can show many people a new and better way of doing things and you can help them achieve many goals.
Girl, 12

I think that being a leader is OK sometimes, but not always. I think once in a while, you should see how other people lead. Maybe to give you ideas in ways you can improve your leadership.
Girl, 13

Leadership is something that you can't push too much. You shouldn't want to be a leader so badly that you take other people's rights and privileges away from them.
Girl, 13

t is hard and frustrating
because you wonder if you made
the right decision.
Girl, 12

I like being a leader, better
than following, because I feel
more responsible, and so, I
work harder.
Girl, 14

Leadership is something that you can't push too much. You shouldn't
want to be a leader so badly that you take other people's rights and
privileges away from them.
Girl, 13

I think if you have leadership abilities, you will probably do well in
life and be good with dealing with people.
Boy, 14

I think I have a positive attitude toward leadership. I think there
should be more leadership training in the community. I believe you
should try to lead others in what you and they believe.
Girl, 13

I think if the liberty isn't
abused, it's great.
Boy, 14

I like the idea that I have finally realized that
being a leader is being able to share a part of
myself with others.
Girl, 14

I would like to be one, but I'm a little bit afraid of failure.
Girl, 15

Being a leader is great, but you
should not concentrate on just
being a leader. You should also
concentrate on being a worker.
Boy, 16

I like to lead others, because I
feel that I can express the
ideas of my followers. I can
organize well, and I never
procrastinate.
Girl, 16

Actions

 # Think About It

Which student has the best attitude toward being a leader? Which attitude is most like yours?

 # Write About It

Write a short essay about your attitude toward being a leader.

Do you think political leaders' attitudes toward leadership affect your attitudes? Are political leaders' attitudes toward leadership changing? If so, do you believe their attitudes are changing in a negative or positive way? Write local, state, and federal politicians for their responses to these questions. Write a statement about this and share it with your friends.

 # Do It

Conduct and analyze a survey of your school class regarding students' attitudes about being a leader. Ask the editor of your school newspaper if the paper can publish the results of your survey. If you don't have a school newspaper, find another way of having it published.

Ask parents about their attitudes toward your being a leader. Did you like what they said? Why or why not?

What would the attitudes toward leadership be of students your age from foreign countries? Write three pen pals from different countries and ask them! Write a short play on attitudes about leadership in other countries and how these compare to attitudes in the United States.

Complete the following statement: I think leadership is important because ...

Conduct a survey in your school or community to determine the differences (if any) in male and female attitudes toward leadership. What impact do you think these differences may have on society in the future?

Ask leaders in your town about their attitudes toward being leaders. How are their attitudes toward leadership alike and how are they different?

What do you think the attitude of your teacher is about your being a leader? Ask! Were you correct?

What do you think the attitudes of the presidents of large companies are toward being leaders? Ask! Were you correct?

● ●

What is your strongest area of leadership skill?

Our survey indicated that the responses may be grouped into three major categories: people-oriented skills, task-oriented skills, and qualities or attributes of leadership. The statements which were more people-oriented were, for the most part, interpersonal skills such as working with others, communicating, motivating people, etc. The task-oriented category consists of responses such as solving problems, thinking logically, finding information, and organizing plans. The qualities of leadership cited as strengths were foresight, innovativeness, confidence, persistence, and persuasiveness.

Ideas

Looking for information
Girl, 10

Knowing what people are saying and understanding what they are trying to tell me without saying anything.
Girl, 10

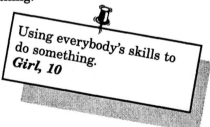

Using everybody's skills to do something.
Girl, 10

I'm determined.
Boy, 10

Being calm in critical times.
Girl, 11

Organizing people and activities well.
Boy, 12

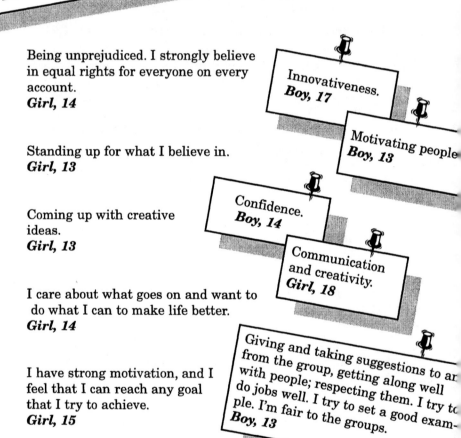

I have an ability to think and react quickly in a situation. I care for people even if they don't care for me. I don't stand back and let people do things for me. I'd rather do them for myself.
Girl, 13

My ability to solve problems.
Girl, 12

Reliability.
Girl, 13

Being unprejudiced. I strongly believe in equal rights for everyone on every account.
Girl, 14

Innovativeness.
Boy, 17

Motivating people
Boy, 13

Standing up for what I believe in.
Girl, 13

Coming up with creative ideas.
Girl, 13

Confidence.
Boy, 14

Communication and creativity.
Girl, 18

I care about what goes on and want to do what I can to make life better.
Girl, 14

I have strong motivation, and I feel that I can reach any goal that I try to achieve.
Girl, 15

Giving and taking suggestions to an from the group, getting along well with people; respecting them. I try to do jobs well. I try to set a good exam-ple. I'm fair to the groups.
Boy, 13

Actions

 # Think About It

How will you use your strengths to be a leader?

What are the strengths of the leaders in your school or community?

Think of your three strongest areas of leadership skills. How might you encourage someone to develop themselves in these areas?

 # Write About It

Write a speech nominating you for the "Great Leaders' Hall of Fame." Include your strengths in leadership.

Write a speech to get elected to a position of your choice in your school or community.

 # Do It

List all of your strengths in leadership skills. Put them in order from the strongest to the weakest. How do you plan to increase those that you consider the weakest? Select a leader whom you admire and list his or her strongest areas of leadership and compare both lists. How are they alike and how are they different?

Collect biographical information on three famous leaders. Analyze the information to determine the strengths of each leader. Compare and contrast these strengths with each of the three leaders and your own.

Develop a leadership logo for yourself incorporating your leadership strengths.

Keeping leadership strengths in mind, comprise an analogy comparing leadership to some non-human item. For example, "A leader is like a sponge because he or she can absorb a great deal of information and put it to good use for the benefit of others," or "A leader is like a lion because it has gained the respect of all other animals through its strength."

What is your weakest area of leadership skill?

Our survey said that many students responded in terms of weaknesses in skills such as decision making, organization, oral and written communication, and delegating. Others spoke of personal characteristics which often keep them from being effective leaders such as procrastination, lack of aggressiveness, inability to accept criticism, lack of patience, inability to admit mistakes, lack of control over emotions, too much concern with trying to please everyone, and too much sensitivity. The responses, in general, showed that the students were very aware of their deficiencies regarding skills necessary for the process of leadership.

Ideas

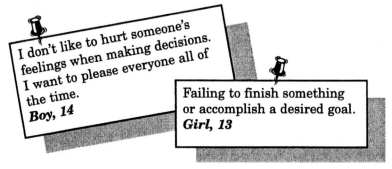

I don't like to hurt someone's feelings when making decisions. I want to please everyone all of the time.
Boy, 14

Failing to finish something or accomplish a desired goal.
Girl, 13

I fly off the handle easily.
Boy, 10

Expressing my feelings and saying what I mean.
Boy, 11

I have trouble admitting I'm wrong.
Girl, 11

Sometimes I leap before I look.
Girl, 12

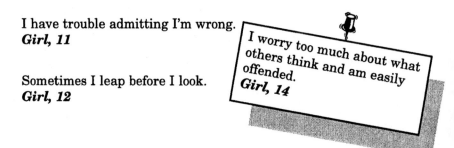

I worry too much about what others think and am easily offended.
Girl, 14

When there are stronger leaders in my group
I kind of fade back.
Boy, 13

My patience. I have a tendency to think others will be able to accomplish tasks as quickly as I can accomplish them myself.
Girl, 17

I've been known to put things off, and even
though it always gets done, I get stressed
trying to get it all done at the last minute.
Girl, 17

Controlling a group.
Boy, 17

Sometimes coming up with new ideas and in some cases
taking criticism.
Boy, 17

My weakest area of leadership skill is probably telling people what
they are doing wrong. I don't have the heart to tell them.
Girl, 18

Actions

💡 Think About It

Is your weakest area the same as any of those given? If not,
what is it?

What do you think were the weakest areas of leadership for
Franklin Delano Roosevelt, Amelia Earhart, Jonas Salk, and John
Glenn. How did they overcome them?

Select a leader you would want to be like. How will you have to
change in order to do this?

Talk About It

Identify and talk with someone in your school or community to help you with your weaknesses in leadership.

Think of a friend who lacks leadership ability. Plan ways that you could help him or her to develop his or her leadership abilities. Can you discuss this with your friend? Be sure to ask him or her for advice on how to improve your leadership abilities.

Interview school, community, or state leaders about what their initial weaknesses were and how they overcame or improved these weakness as a leader.

Get a group of three or four of your friends together and have each person list three strengths and three weaknesses (in terms of leadership abilities) for each person in the group. Swap lists so that each person has his or her own lists of strengths and weaknesses. Discuss them with your friends if you feel comfortable with this.

 Write About It

Keep a diary or log of particularly weak areas of leadership you would like to strengthen. Make a record of your behavior and actions as you work toward improving them.

 Think about three weak areas of leadership which you would like to work on. Develop strategies for improving your weak areas.

Do It

What will you do about your weakest area? Develop a plan to make your weakest area into a strength in leadership. Write your goal, objectives, resource person(s), and a timeline.

What other areas would you like to strengthen? Develop additional plans.

Write a comedy skit on how one must overcome weaknesses in leadership. Get your friends to join you and present it to your class!

Draw a cartoon strip showing what may happen to weak leaders.

Make a list of the changes that you would like to make in your leadership abilities. Design a progress chart that you will follow for the next week, month, or year.

Role play situations in which a leader must be assertive. Identify assertive behaviors that you would like to have and practice them.

Role play a situation in which you as a leader must admit a mistake to your group.

Think of ways to convince your group members to successfully complete a project. Try them out!

Make a list of your weaknesses as a leader. For each area you consider to be a weakness, determine two or three strategies for improving in those areas. Ask an adult who is close to you to look at your ideas and discuss them with you.

Chapter 3
Opportunities for Leadership

What opportunities do you have for being a leader in your school?

Our survey said that the majority of students saw many opportunities for being a leader in their schools. Opportunities included those associated with student councils, sports, fine and performing arts, and academics. A few students gave examples for opportunities for leadership within the classroom.

Ideas

Giving assistance or help, setting good examples, following the rules, and doing your work.
Boy, 12

I've got opportunities by being in Girl Scouts and by being a good speaker.
Girl, 9

When we do small group projects.
Boy, 10

In school we sometimes have group reports for which we need leaders, sports teams, after school clubs, and contests.
Girl, 12

There are lots of opportunities to be a leader in my school. The main ones I like are Student Council, class newspaper, class plays, and the Ideas Program (enrichment class).
Boy, 12

An opportunity to become a leader is open for almost everyone, if you have satisfactory grades and citizenship.
Girl, 13

There are lots of clubs including: drama, newspaper, foreign language, student council, etc., in which you can establish yourself. Also, you can establish yourself with your friends and be a leader.
Girl, 14

> I get the opportunity to express the views of my fellow classmates, to make a difference in my school, and to do the job which people who believe in me trust me to do.
> *Boy, 16*

Student council, band council, and other things like this, but most are just popularity contests.
Boy, 14

The opportunity that I have for being a leader in my school is involvement in student council. To serve a purpose for awareness and to communicate with the whole school. Many club officer positions have helped benefit my leadership skills which helped me to become better situated as a role model.
Girl, 18

Actions

♀ Think About It

What other opportunities for being a leader in your school would you like to have? How could you help develop more opportunities?

Some people believe that leaders are chosen because they are popular. What do you think? Are your school leaders chosen only because they are popular. If so, what could be done to change the system so that those with the most leadership ability would be elected?

What is the difference between an elected leader and a leader who emerges in a group activity? In what ways could you be a leader in your school other than being elected or appointed?

Write About It

Write an article for the school newspaper or prepare a speech about the opportunities for being a leader in your school.

Do It

Hold a meeting for other students who might like to have additional opportunities for leadership in the school. As a group, write a brief proposal outlining why you would like more opportunities for leadership and give examples of additional opportunities you would like to have incorporated in your school. Arrange for a meeting with interested parents, school board members, administrators, counselors, and teachers to discuss your proposal.

Give your school principal a "Recipe for Leadership." The recipe should include a step-by-step approach to developing the leadership of students in your school.

Using past school annuals or other printed material which may be available through your principal, create a historical diagram of the clubs, organizations, and other opportunities for leadership that have been offered in your school since it began. How have these opportunities changed? Are there more or fewer opportunities now? Analyze the progression of these opportunities in your school and write a brief report to present to your principal, faculty, school board, etc.

Design a survey to send to friends and relatives who attend schools other than yours. Ask that they list all opportunities for leadership in their school and return the form to you. Make a composite list of potential leadership opportunities in your school and compare it to the list of opportunities you have received from other schools. How are they alike? How are they different? Are there opportunities for leadership in other schools that could be used in your school?

Analyze the responsibilities of the presidents of all the clubs and organizations in your school. Do all have the same duties? Which ones are the most effective? How can the others become more effective?

Make a list of all the scholastic and sports leadership positions in your school and the responsibilities of each. Circle the ones that are most important to you. Develop a step-by-step guide for yourself for being a leader in your school.

Complete the following statement. I want to be a leader in my school because ...

Brainstorm a list of elected positions in school and ways that a person can be a leader in school without being elected.

● ●

What opportunities do you have for being a leader in your community?

Our survey said that students gave many examples such as organized youth clubs and associations, community projects, and their jobs. A few students were able to develop their own, self-initiated opportunities for leadership by developing new clubs and organizations within their communities.

Ideas

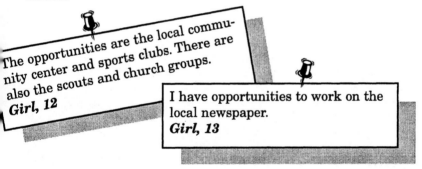

The opportunities are the local community center and sports clubs. There are also the scouts and church groups.
Girl, 12

I have opportunities to work on the local newspaper.
Girl, 13

Leader in clubs such as Clean-up committee and Crime Watch.
Girl, 12

Community projects, baby-sitting.
Girl, 13

Holding block parties, starting your own business, charity committees.
Girl, 13

An officer in 4-H.
Girl, 15

Candy-striping
Girl, 15

Opportunities I have are becoming involved in city band, YMCA, and service organization such as United Fund, March of Dimes, etc. I also have the opportunity to be a leader in summer youth programs in the community.
Girl, 17

In the community, I have been exposed to leadership opportunities numerous times through my work.
Boy, 16

Many—you just have to go out and find them. Groups and organizations are best for this.
Boy, 17

In the community there are such things as Mayor's Youth Advisory Board, church organizations, and special interest groups like civic theater.
Boy, 16

I belong to Girl Scouts in which I've had a lot of leadership experience not only with kids but also adults. All of the adults know my reputation and trust me to come through for them. I've run a lot of projects and help lead even if I'm not in charge.
Girl, 13

I started a track team for youth in the community.
Girl, 17

Every city has opportunities for young people to be leaders, and my city or community is no different. We have Boy Scouts and Girl Scouts which are filled with leadership opportunities. Since I live in a capital city, this also brings about opportunities to work with mayors, governors, and other government people. The youth organizations provide super opportunities for students and young people to become leaders.
Boy, 18

Actions

Think About It

Do you have the same opportunities as those listed? If not, how are they different?

What opportunities are there for being a leader in your community?

Write About It

Write a letter to the editor of your local newspaper outlining the reasons why more youth leadership opportunities should be provided in your community. Be sure to be positive and suggest ways this might happen.

Brainstorm a list of elected leadership positions for youth in the community and ways young people can be leaders in the community without being elected.

Do It

If you need more information about the possibility of leadership opportunities for students in your community, ask your counselor or call the office of your mayor or Chamber of Commerce and ask.

Complete the following statement. I want to be a leader in my community because ...

Make a list of the things that you would like to begin or change in your community. Make a plan to lead in one or more of these areas.

Conduct a poll of your friends in other communities to determine the opportunities for being a leader. Make a composite list of the potential leadership opportunities in your community and compare it to the list you have received from other communities. How are they alike? How are they different? Are there opportunities for leadership in other communities that could be used in your community?

Contact three influential community leaders and tell them about the need for more leadership opportunities for youth. Ask for their help in taking action toward this goal.

Contact community leaders in art, politics, education, business, and industry. Develop interview questions for them such as who or what influenced them to be leaders, what advice would they give to young leaders, and how do they see leadership changing for the future, etc. Use this information to develop an audio- or videotape, a booklet, or some other product that could be given to students in the community.

For history buffs, trace the early leaders in your community and develop, in print form, a historical overview of the early influences of community leaders as well as how community leadership has changed.

Make a collage of the way early leaders influenced major developments in the community.

Develop a list of community leaders who would like to be mentors (guides) to young leaders and organize a mentor experience for students of your age.

Develop a list of part-time jobs in your community that have opportunities for leadership and share it with others.

● ●

What opportunities do you have for being a leader in your church or religious affiliation?

Our survey said that students view their church or religious affiliation as providing a wide range of opportunities for being a leader. They included direct contact with those of their own ages to serving on committees and boards with adults. Sponsored events within and outside the church or religious affiliation also offered opportunities.

Ideas

Speaking in front of the congregation and in Sunday School.
Girl, 11

Our class made decorations, planned entertainment, acted, and fixed dinner all by ourselves.
Girl, 12

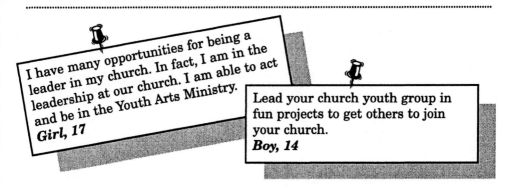

I have many opportunities for being a leader in my church. In fact, I am in the leadership at our church. I am able to act and be in the Youth Arts Ministry.
Girl, 17

Lead your church youth group in fun projects to get others to join your church.
Boy, 14

Working in the nursery and showing I can handle situations.
Girl, 13

The opportunity for being a leader in my church is the Royal Ambassadors which is a youth group which contributes time in the community to help others.
Girl, 18

Help coordinate Sunday School programs.
Boy, 14

Youth Council, working at Vacation Bible School, planning activities, setting a good example.
Girl, 14

Many, there is the church council and many boards that run my church, and teenagers are welcome on all of them.
Girl, 16

Actions

Think About It

What leadership opportunities in your religious affiliation appeal to you? Complete the following statement. I want to be a leader in my religious affiliation because ...

Think of other opportunities that could be started.

Talk About It

Talk with the head of your religious affiliation to get his or her ideas on leadership activities in which you can be involved.

Write About It

Write an article for your religious affiliation bulletin or newsletter about the need for more leadership activities for kids.

 Do It

Call your friends who attend other religious organizations. Make a list of leadership opportunities that are available for young persons in other religious organizations.

 Brainstorm a list of leadership activities you would like available in your religious affiliation. Circle the one you think is the most important. Write a plan for getting this activity started.

Compare the list to leadership opportunities in your religious affiliation. How are they alike? How are they different? Are there opportunities for leadership in other religious institutions that could be used in your religious affiliation? Brainstorm a list of elected positions of leadership for young persons in your religious affiliation and ways a young person can be a leader in your religious affiliation without being elected.

Design activities for younger students to encourage them to become leaders in their religious affiliation.

Chapter 4
Training for Leadership

What opportunities do you have for training in leadership concepts and skills in your school (i.e., special classes, after school programs, workshops, etc.)?

Our survey stated that students had several sources of training for leadership within their schools. The most typical examples were student council, special clubs, and programs for high ability and gifted students. Summer programs focused on leadership training were available to a few students. Some students perceive training as being unavailable or limited in their schools.

Ideas

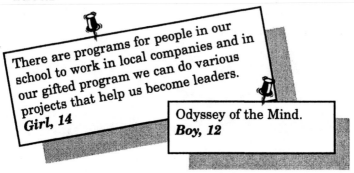

There are programs for people in our school to work in local companies and in our gifted program we can do various projects that help us become leaders.
Girl, 14

Odyssey of the Mind.
Boy, 12

Special classes, Girl Scouts, and Safety Patrol.
Girl, 11

Leadership class and Student Council.
Girl, 12

Workshops and Student Council.
Girl, 13

Student government, leadership class, and clubs.
Girl, 13

Leadership Week.
Boy, 14

Mostly through the study of history and psychology. History shows how past leaders have performed, and psychology helps to understand the needs of others as well as myself.
Girl, 17

I'm able to be involved in a mentorship with a community professional, advanced classes in English and Biology, Future Problem Solving, varsity sports, and a multitude of organizations and clubs such as National Honor Society, French Club, and Students Against Driving Drunk.
Girl, 17

I have attended a leadership program at a university in the summer.
Girl, 14

We, in some classes, have been exposed to leadership type concepts; unfortunately, these opportunities have been few and far between.
Boy, 16

Leadership workshop, speech and debate classes.
Girl, 15

Debate.
Boy, 16

Actions

💡 Think About It

Do you have more or fewer opportunities than the ones given?
What other opportunities would you like to have available?
In which opportunities would you like to participate?

✎ Write About It

Write a short puppet show or play about teachers assisting students in developing their leadership skills.

Compile a directory of opportunities for leadership development in your school. Publish the results in your school newspaper.

☞ Do It

Present your puppet show or play at a faculty meeting or another appropriate group of educators. Use humor as much as possible while expressing your important message of the need for more leadership training in the classroom.

Contact your principal, teacher, or guidance counselor and tell him or her about the kind of leadership development you would like to have in your school and offer to help plan the training.

Set up a school resource file of the names, addresses, and phone numbers of adult leaders who would be willing to devote time to training students in leadership concepts and skills.

Organize an after school leadership club in which you may read about and discuss famous leaders as well as leadership concepts and skills. Use the reading list.

●●●●●●●●●●●●●●●●●●●●●●●●●●●●●●●●

What opportunities do you have for training in leadership concepts and skills in your community (i.e., workshops, seminars, etc.)?

Our survey said that students in some communities have a variety of opportunities for leadership training available to them. Others appear to have created their own opportunities, while a few stated that there were none. Opportunities focused on those associated with clubs for students, participation with adults, and special situations which community leaders have established for youth.

Ideas

I get to lead in clubs that my friends and I make.
Boy, 10

My friends and I have an exercise and dance club, and I'm one of the leaders.
Girl, 10

I have club and team opportunities, and I am the oldest kid on the block.
Girl, 11

Volunteer, junior firefighter.
Boy, 13

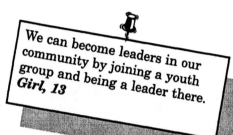

We can become leaders in our community by joining a youth group and being a leader there.
Girl, 13

I organized a fund raiser for the starving people in Ethiopia.
Boy, 18

Actions

💡 Think About It

What generalizations or conclusions can you think of that are reflected in the responses about leadership training in the community?

What ideas can you and your friends come up with to motivate the adults in your community to help you get started in leadership development programs? See the mayor? Go to a banker? See your city librarian?

👉 Do It

What kinds of youth leadership training programs exist in your community? Develop a resource file.

Identify influential leaders in your community. Get a group of other students interested in leadership development with adult leaders. Ask for their help in determining and implementing leadership training programs for youth. This may take a good bit of research on your part, but there are programs available!

Design a plan for leadership training for students younger than you. Get other youth leaders involved in helping you plan and implement your program. Be sure to get input from adult leaders before beginning this project as well as feedback on evaluation of the project after it has been completed.

Conduct a survey of leadership training activities in your community and make a chart showing the results of the survey. Send it to your local paper and to your school newspaper. Ask to be on a television or radio talk show to give these results. If there are not many existing leadership training programs, ask the television and radio audiences to offer ideas and assistance in developing such programs.

Conduct an analysis of existing leadership training programs. Who may attend the programs? What ages are the participants? What are the costs, if any? What are the goals and objectives of the program? Present this information to your local Chamber of Commerce or similar organization.

List the community leadership training programs in which you have been involved. State the positive and negative aspects of these programs. Develop a handbook of the ones you would recommend.

Contact local businesses in your community to determine the types of leadership training programs available for employees. Get their input on how these programs might be adapted for youth.

Develop a petition and get signatures from kids and their parents who are interested in leadership training programs. Present it to the mayor or city manager and ask for a city-wide youth leadership training program.

● ●

What opportunities do you have for training in leadership concepts and skills in your church or religious affiliation (i.e., workshops, seminars, etc.)?

Our survey said that students stated that leadership training is generally available through church and religious affiliations. Special seminars and workshops on leadership training are offered in many religious affiliations and some students receive special leadership training in religious organization camps for youth.

Ideas

The opportunities I have for training in leadership concepts and skills in my church are Sunday School, church choir, helping with the service, church summer camp, and youth group.
Boy, 10

A seminar held every month on Saturdays.
Girl, 13

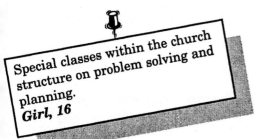

Talking in front of the church congregation, talking in front of youth groups, showing new and different ways to do things.
Boy, 14

You can go to Sunday School and learn about the leaders of the past and how they led people.
Girl, 13

Special classes within the church structure on problem solving and planning.
Girl, 16

Our church sometimes has seminars about leadership.
Girl, 14

Actions

♀ Think About It

Most religious affiliations depend on the youth to help add enthusiasm and variety to the religious affiliation family. How could you and other youth in your religious affiliation convince the adults that youth leadership training programs will help to develop and strengthen programs and will benefit your organization in many ways?

👉 Do It

Contact some of your friends and adult leaders in your religious organization. As a group, brainstorm ways for providing more training for leadership concepts and skills through various activities such as Sunday School, Hebrew School, choir, youth group, study or religious writings, etc.

Plan a leadership lock-in for the youth of your religious organization. Organize activities which would get kids involved in skills of leadership such as speaking in front of a group, group problem solving, planning youth projects, etc. Discuss famous religious leaders. Select five famous religious leaders (past or present) and do research on their backgrounds. What leadership styles do/did they use? How do you feel they can be/could have been more effective as leaders. Write stories about these leaders for the younger children in your religious organization. Plan a time to present the stories to these children.

If you could change society's attitude toward religion, what would you like to change, and how would you go about it?

Survey members of your religious organization to determine those that could design a leadership training program for youth. Ask them to meet with you and develop a timeline for beginning the training activities.

Select a religious leader (past or present) that you consider to be your role model. Write a letter to this person explaining why he or she is a role model for you. Send it to the person if he or she is still alive, but be sure to keep a copy for yourself!

Chapter 5
Influence and Encouragement
from Others

Who or what has had the most influence on the development of your leadership abilities and why?

Our survey said that family members, teachers and other school personnel, friends, and religious leaders were most often named as those influencing the leadership development of these youth. Participation in programs, caring for pets, and others have also influenced leadership abilities. Although the reasons offered were many, there were several frequently given. They were serving as role models, developing responsibility, acquiring speaking skills, and believing in the students' abilities.

Ideas

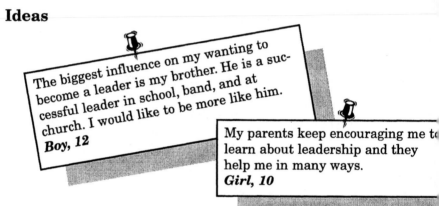

The biggest influence on my wanting to become a leader is my brother. He is a successful leader in school, band, and at church. I would like to be more like him.
Boy, 12

My parents keep encouraging me to learn about leadership and they help me in many ways.
Girl, 10

My art teacher, she told me never to quit on something.
Boy, 10

My mother always encouraged me to try new things and to get more involved in my school and to run for student council.
Girl, 12

My father because he taught me to take the initiative and do things.
Boy, 12

My fourth grade teacher because he told me to get out and meet new people and to speak my ideas.
Boy, 11

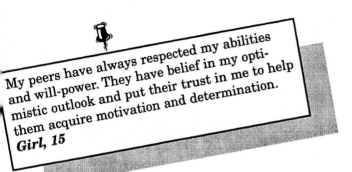

My peers have always respected my abilities and will-power. They have belief in my optimistic outlook and put their trust in me to help them acquire motivation and determination.
Girl, 15

My teacher has influenced my development of leadership abilities because he has taught us to be responsible and to help peers.
Girl, 13

The Leadership Camp. It taught me a lot about how to be a leader.
Girl, 13

Older scouts in the troop showed me how to organize and control groups.
Boy, 14

My parents and teachers give me intelligence, good judgment, wisdom, and responsibility.
Boy, 13

My dog, cats, and bunnies—they teach me responsibility and they give me love back.
Girl, 14

My mother, she is a leader, too. I always hear her planning all kinds of things.
Girl, 14

My participation in the debate team. It has taught me to be assertive and less shy about public speaking.
Boy, 16

Being in clubs, on the debate team, and in the program for gifted students.
Boy, 16

My friends have had the most influence on my development of leadership abilities. I started getting involved by following their good examples as leaders.
Girl, 17

My mom. She's always encouraged me to do whatever I feel is right. She taught me responsibility and to be an individual.
Girl, 17

Actions

Think About It

Who has most influenced your leadership abilities?

What book or situation has had the most influence on your leadership abilities?

Select a leader from the past and think about his or her influence on you if you had lived during that period of time. Does he or she influence you now? How?

What person or persons have discouraged you from developing as a leader? How have they been obstacles to your leadership development?

Read About It

Read a biography or an autobiography of a leader and determine who influenced him or her in leadership.

How can parents best encourage leadership concepts and skills in their children?

Our survey said that many suggestions were given as to how parents can best encourage leadership. Some of the suggestions were the giving of responsibility in the home, allowing decision making on the part of students, listening to their ideas, and encouraging them to be leaders and to participate in school, community, and religious events. Students also stated that parents should praise them when they accomplish their goals. They also wanted parents to provide leadership training activities for them outside of the home by allowing the students to attend training programs and seminars.

Ideas

They can praise their children for their accomplishments and build their self-confidence.
Girl, 14

My parents don't encourage me.
Boy, 10

They can have us read and study up on being a leader.
Girl, 10

They can show their children how to cope with their problems.
Girl, 14

By giving them problem solving questions.
Boy, 13

By believing in them and helping them.
Girl, 14

Parents can best encourage leadership by talking over problems and pointing out our mistakes.
Girl, 10

By taking part in community events and helping their kids also get involved.
Girl, 12

Teach them to communicate and express themselves. Don't hinder those things. Give them responsibility.
Girl, 17

● ●

Actions

💡 Think About It

What are your parents doing to encourage you to be a leader? What else would you like them to do?

👉 Do It

Talk with your parents about leadership and leaders. Do they know leaders you could talk to about being a leader? Think of questions that you would like to ask leaders. Call the person(s) and make an appointment.

Developing responsibility is an important part of leadership. What responsibilities do you have in your family? Which ones do you want in the future to help you be a leader? Talk to your parents about new responsibilities and when you will begin.

Make a list of persons who have already influenced you as a leader and how they have done so.

Make a list of persons who could have an influence on your leadership abilities in the future. How could they help you?

Brainstorm the ways you think you will help your child become a leader. Write a letter to the child you hope to have and tell him or her about this.

Talk with your parents about allowing you to plan some of the following activities: a meal, a party, a family vacation, a shopping trip, a family visit to a local nursing home, etc. Other fun family activities you may want to plan are collecting toys and books for children in the hospital, and organizing magazine collections for nursing homes. Use your imagination and your local resources!

Have you read something about a famous leader and his or her parents' influence that you would like to share with your parents?

Get a group of your friends together. Design short skits that portray parents in opposite ways; situations in which parents do not encourage their children to be leaders and situations in which parents do encourage their children to be leaders. Present your skits to various groups of kids and parents.

Get several friends together and prepare brief written statements describing why you think it's important for you to gain leadership concepts and skills. Arrange a meeting at your home or school for parents. Present your ideas and discuss the positive aspects of leadership for kids.

● ●

How can teachers best encourage leadership concepts and skills in their students?

Our survey said that students gave many suggestions on how teachers could best encourage leadership concepts and skills. Teachers should create environments in their classrooms which allow students to take more responsibility and build their self-confidence. Through discussions, students want to develop their thinking and creativity skills and become better speakers. Teachers should encourage students to be leaders and indicate the positive aspects of leadership. Students also said they would like information on school and club elections and opportunities to attend programs and seminars on leadership.

Ideas

By giving leadership roles in the classes and more responsibility.
Boy, 12

They talk about it and take time out for it.
Girl, 10

By encouraging working in groups during class.
Boy, 14

Teach something about leadership in their classes.
Girl, 11

By showing them their strengths and strengthening their weaknesses.
Girl, 14

Many teachers ask questions and insist on only one possible answer. Teachers need to listen to students' ideas even if they are not always quite right.
Girl, 14

Be a model, encourage risk-taking, study leadership skills.
Girl, 17

Teaching them that it's good to be a leader.
Boy, 15

Put them in situations where they must use these concepts and skills.
Girl, 16

Teachers can encourage leadership concepts and skills to their children by talking to their children about leadership. Also to have a positive attitude about leadership and how much you're able to get out of all the goals you set for yourself.
Boy, 17

Make sure the student works up to potential.
Girl, 16

They can have leaders come to the classes and talk about leadership concepts and skills.
Girl, 17

Actions

Think About It

Think of all the ways you could be a leader in your classroom and discuss these with your teacher. Ask him or her to help you develop more responsibilities.

Write About It

Write an editorial for your school newspaper on how teachers can and should promote leadership skills for youth.

Compose a song about teachers and leadership in the classroom.

 Do It

Talk to your teacher, guidance counselor, or principal about the ways to demonstrate leadership in your school through clubs and groups. Make a list and decide which one you would like to join.

Think of a teacher who allows students to have some responsibilities within class. Seek his or her assistance in designing a plan of action for getting other teachers in your school to help students become more responsible leaders.

Hold an election of the teachers in your grade. Have the students select the teacher who best encourages leadership development.

Make a list of the ways your teachers encourage leadership. Write to other students across the country and compare your responses to theirs.

Design a poster listing the positive things that teachers do to promote leadership in their classrooms. Design another poster listing the things that teachers do to prevent leadership in their classrooms.

Give a monthly award to the teacher who best promotes leadership in the classroom.

Chapter 6
Great Leaders

Who do you consider to be one of the greatest leaders of all times (past and present)? Why?

Our survey said that the names of political and governmental leaders were commonly offered as the greatest leaders, past and present, by the students. There were a few females viewed as being leaders. The majority of the leaders were of the past and not of the present. Interestingly, one girl perceived her parents to be the greatest leaders.

Ideas

Julius Caesar—Because of the way he lead the Roman Empire, by making sure that the people followed him. He was an army leader, a statesman, a reformer, and a writer. He conquered present day France and invaded England.
Girl, 12

William Clark and Merriweather Lewis—With their courageous exploration of the new Louisiana Purchase.
Boy, 10

John F. Kennedy—Because he could really talk to the people and not at them. He could really persuade people in what he was talking about.
Boy, 10

Harriet Tubman—Because she led blacks out of slavery.
Boy, 11

Ghandi—Because he used peace instead of violence to lead.
Boy, 12

Franklin Roosevelt—He, being in a wheelchair, led us through the Great Depression and also was the only U.S. president who stayed in office four terms.
Girl, 12

Jesus Christ—Because he created one of the greatest movements of all time and led by example and sacrificed his life for his ideals.
Boy, 16

My parents.
Girl, 14

Ghandi—He always stood by what he knew was right and never compromised his beliefs; that's why people followed him.
Girl, 14

Martin Luther King Jr.—Because he had the courage to defy traditions and do what was right.
Girl, 14

Mother Theresa—She leads people in helping others—she takes charge in what she's doing.
Girl, 13

Abraham Lincoln—He brought the blacks out of slavery in that he put them ahead of himself. I think he was a great man for being so humble.
Girl, 15

Winston Churchill—He became the spirit of his country in a time of great need. He responded to troubled times with charismatic sternness that the situation necessitated.
Boy, 17

Adolph Hitler—Although I heartily disapprove of what he did, he had great leadership qualities. He got what he wanted done.
Girl, 16

Florence Nightingale—Because she did what no one else did, because she wanted to help others.
Girl, 17

Actions

 # Think About It

Who do you consider to be one of the greatest leaders of all times and why?

What generalizations or big, connecting ideas could you make from the students' responses?

How does your response compare to the students' responses?

Are there other great religious leaders? What were their contributions?

Think of leaders who changed our lives but may not be known to many people.

It has often been said that a civilization can be described by a study of its moral and religious leaders? Do you agree or disagree? Can you think of specific examples?

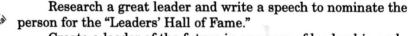 Write About It

Write a story and create leaders of the future based on a futuristic need and get it published in the school or local newspaper.

 Research a great leader and write a speech to nominate the person for the "Leaders' Hall of Fame."

Create a leader of the future in one area of leadership and write a play, skit, song, or story to be shared with young children.

Create riddles or puzzles about great leaders. Put them in a book for your friends.

Write an essay entitled, "The Best Leader I've Ever Known." Ask your principal to let you read it at the next school program. Ask your principal, English teacher, or mayor to sponsor an essay contest on the same or similar topics.

Do It

Create a scrapbook, diorama, mobile, or some other visual representation of a great leader.

Research great leaders to determine how their families fostered leadership ability. Share these ideas with your parents.

Research leaders and categorize them according to their leadership style (democratic, autocratic, *laissez faire*).

Research how great leaders build a power base and relate this to your goals for leadership.

Research leaders and tell why the person is considered a great leader, then develop a booklet for younger students.

Research a leader of the past and predict how the person would function on a current issue. Examples: How would Abraham Lincoln solve apartheid in South Africa? How would Michelangelo help society become more art literate?

Research and compare the similarities and differences between leaders who had/have a negative influence on society with those who had/have a positive influence.

Make a scrapbook of great leaders by collecting photographs and biographical information on leaders from the past and present.

Have a "Great Leaders Party" at your home or in school. Everyone comes dressed as a great leader but does not reveal who he or she is. As you talk with each other at the party you may ask questions that require a "yes" or "no" response in order to guess the identity of each person.

Using books, journals, and information about great leaders of the past and present, complete the "Leadership Matrix" on page 166. Be sure to include female and male, as well as those from different ethnic and religious backgrounds.

Chapter 7
Advice to Others

What is the best advice you could give to someone who wants to become a leader?

Our survey indicated that responses show great depth and insight. Many students suggested training in leadership such as attending workshops, seminars, and classes. Others recommended reading books about leadership and researching past leaders, observing and following role models, and becoming involved in extracurricular activities.

Some students advised those who want to become leaders to work on weaknesses and build strengths, listen to and try to understand the group with which they work, and to be positive and believe in themselves. A few students cautioned potential leaders against being too pushy or obnoxious. They also warned others not to be conceited in leadership positions and not to lose sight of what it feels like to be a follower.

Ideas

I'd tell them to always be prepared and to be sure of what they want to do and be sure they want to devote their time to the job.
Girl, 12

Learn how to express ideas openly and how to communicate with people.
Girl, 11

Think before you speak, don't criticize unless you are perfect yourself.
Girl, 10

Do research about being a leader.
Girl, 10

I would tell them that in order to be a good leader you have to accept a lot of responsibilities and always listen to what your followers have to say.
Girl, 12

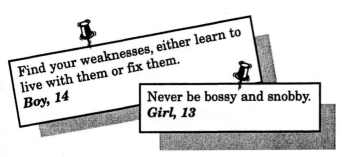

Find your weaknesses, either learn to live with them or fix them.
Boy, 14

Never be bossy and snobby.
Girl, 13

Believe in what you are doing and be worthy of the respect of others.
Girl, 11

To have people follow you, you can't be pushy or obnoxious, because even if they trust your abilities and ideas, they won't want to follow a person they don't like. To be a good leader, you have to listen to other people's ideas and thoughts about things and can't be conceited. Leaders also must be willing to change their ideas at times and admit it if they're wrong.
Girl, 13

Take a leadership class or workshop.
Boy, 12

Keep trying until you become one.
Girl, 13

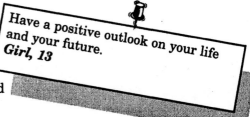

Have a positive outlook on your life and your future.
Girl, 13

Being a leader comes from inside you. If you want to be a leader, step out and do what you think is right and don't give up.
Boy, 12

Trust in yourself and take the initiative.
Boy, 13

Watch and observe one of your favorite leaders.
Girl, 14

Go some place where you can improve leadership skills.
Boy, 14

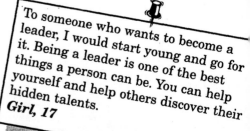

To someone who wants to become a leader, I would start young and go for it. Being a leader is one of the best things a person can be. You can help yourself and help others discover their hidden talents.
Girl, 17

Improve your weaknesses and build your strengths.
Boy, 15

Read about leaders, try to find one role model. Read self-improvement books. It takes time to become a leader. Take your path and don't let anyone else tell you what to think.
Girl, 15

Attend workshops and seminars. Become involved with extracurricular activities.
Boy, 16

Assert yourself, be dependable, don't try to do it all. Delegate authority.
Boy, 16

To practice your leadership skills is the only way to learn. Trial and error.
Girl, 16

• •

Actions

 # Think About It

Select the statements which best describe the advice you would give someone. What makes it the best advice?

Is there other advice that you would give a person wanting to be a leader?

Develop a motto or a saying which states the advice that you would give someone about being a leader.

What is the best advice that you can give yourself on becoming a leader?

Many quotes on leadership have been provided for you in this book. Which ones are the most representative of advice you think is best?

What advice do you think our present president would give for becoming a leader?

Do It

Close your eyes and picture yourself as a leader in six months or a year. Keep your eyes closed and continue to think about your leadership position when you finish college. Make a list of the kinds of leadership positions that you would like to have in your community, school, or religious affiliation in the next five years.

Survey other students in your school to get their ideas on the best advice for someone wanting to become a leader. Design a poster of this advice and display it in the hallway.

Survey adult leaders in your school, community, or religious affiliation to get their ideas on the best advice for someone wanting to become a leader. Design a poster of this advice. Compare the students' advice to the adults' advice. How are they alike? How are they different?

Choose five great leaders and develop a skit based on the advice that they would give on becoming a leader.

Write, produce, and videotape a television commercial for leadership encouraging younger students to become leaders. Present the commercial to your local television station. Be creative with your message of the importance of leadership!

Create a new game on "How to become a leader." Think of all the "setbacks" or "obstacles" that a leader may face. This may make your game more interesting!

Individual and Group
Leadership Accomplishments

Brain Power for Kids

Her vision is to revolutionize global education. Her name is Lana Israel, currently a freshman at Harvard University. Lana's interest in education was piqued at the age of 13, when her father suggested that she read Tony Buzan's book, *Use Both Sides of Your Brain*. He claimed that it was interesting and thought that Lana could gain some good ideas from the book. Lana commented, "At the age of 13, reading a book because my dad deemed it 'interesting' was as foreign to me as snorkeling at the Great Barrier Reef." The next summer Lana was snorkeling at the Great Barrier Reef. For she had read the book and from it learned about mind mapping, a holistic learning technique. Extremely interested in the possibility of applying mind mapping to education, rather than industry and business, Lana turned mind mapping to her eighth grade science project. She received fascinating results, and it was suggested by Lana's elementary school gifted teacher that she apply to speak at the Eighth World Conference on Gifted and Talented Children in Sydney, Australia. Lana was invited as the only child lecturer to present her research, and she was actually able to go snorkeling at the Great Barrier Reef.

In preparation for the conference, Lana had written a book on mind mapping, *Brain Power for Kids: How to Become an Instant Genius*, which she intended to distribute to the educators attending her presentation. In Australia, Lana fell the delighted victim to Australia's press and soon found her photo being distributed around the continent in national newspapers, her voice being heard on national radio, and found herself on the sets of television shows such as Good Morning Australia, 'Till 10, and The Ray Martin Show. The result was a publishing deal with Hawker-Brownlow publishers.

Lana returned to normality and her Miami home that summer, only to find a business kit her father had ordered for her from a company called Business Kids. The kit taught young people how to become entrepreneurs and was in immediate interest to Lana who had also been enthusiastic about entrepreneurship. By the time she completed the kit, she came across a minor obstacle: none of the suggested businesses appealed to her. She soon realized, however, that there was no need to start a business because she was already running one. She recalled the demand for the information she was presenting in Australia and realized that she didn't have to only hand out her books at conferences but could begin to sell them herself. Thus, Brain Power for Kids Inc. was born and Lana self-published her book in the United States. Today she has sold more than 10,000 copies and awaits the printing of her next book, *Learning How to Learn Math*.

She returned home to another surprise, a call from Tony Buzan's office. Lana had sent a copy of her eighth grade science project on mind mapping to his London office. She was in awe after receiving an invitation for her family and her to join him for lunch in Palm Beach Fl. That one lunch began the start of a wonderful relationship. Tony and Lana have appeared on educational programs and lectured together. He has co-authored the recent editions of *Brain Power for Kids*, and they continually work together on various projects. Lana has also continued to conduct scientific research on learning methodologies, specifically mind mapping, in search of validation for her books and the ability to enhance the state of education. She recently completed "The Unlimited Mind: A Five-Year Study," which is a cumulative report on her research and is to be published in *Synapsia: The International Brain Journal*. Lana also writes a column, "Young Business Brain," for the journal.

As the developer and founder of *Brain Power for Kids*, Lana lectures to parents, students, and teachers internationally. After her trip to Australia she was booked for several speaking engagements by individuals who had been at the conference and also lived in Florida. Soon, word of mouth and press coverage led to numerous bookings for Lana worldwide. She was selected by Business Kids to lecture in Moscow at the First Businessship Symposium. Her achievements as a young business leader led Lana to be named Seventeen Magazine's Entrepreneur of 1990 and to an appearance on Good Morning America. Lana has also lectured in South Africa, Belgium, England, Scotland, Wales, and at the Ninth World Conference for Gifted and Talented Children in the Netherlands.

In 1993, she won the Grand Award at the 44th International Science and Engineering Fair in Gulfport, Mississippi. This award, The Glenn T. Seaborg Nobel Prize Visit Award, is a one week visit to Stockholm, Sweden, to attend the Nobel Prizes, which she attended in December of that year. She also won first place in the Division of

Social and Behavioral Sciences, and four special awards. In total she received six awards for her research.

Last year, Lana was asked to star in a 60-minute video, *Get Ahead*, which focuses on test-taking strategies and mind mapping. After winning numerous awards, the video has become a big hit in the United Kingdom and may soon be released in the United States. "I absolutely love what I do," explains Lana. "My work gives me the best of business, writing, public speaking, scientific research, public relations, publishing, video." On March 26, 1994, she was named the co-winner of the Brain of the Year Award in London. The award is given by a British charity called the Brain Trust. She shared the award with two time World Memory Champion Dominic O'Brien. Past winners include Stephen Hawking, Gene Roddenberry, and Garry Kasparov.

Lana has also assumed various leadership roles in school. She was class president since her sophomore year, served as both treasurer and squad leader for debate, vice president of the Science Honor Society, and president of her school's Technology Student Association, just to name a few. She was also a member of her high school's soccer, cross country, track, volleyball, and softball teams, and was the fourth leading scorer in soccer in her district. She has also served as the chair of the City of North Miami Beach Youth Advisory Board for two consecutive years. Lana Israel certainly understands the meaning of leadership and hopes to continue in her endeavors and lead us all into a new decade of education.

The GreenKids

GreenKids was established during the 1990-1991 school year. The sixth grade students at Lafayette Regional School in rural Franconia, NH, started the project as part of an integrated subject, Critical Skills L.B.R.P. (Learning by Real Problems). The students knew of the absence of a children's environmental project in New England and they wanted to alleviate the problems of the environment.

The first group of students, "First Generation GreenKids," brainstormed and came up with a list of goals that they hoped to achieve during that school year. Goals included establishing the group, writing a "Book of Issues, For Kids By Kids," having it published, writing a quarterly newsletter, promoting recycling and responsible environmental attitudes throughout the area, and finally, showing that adults will listen to the opinions of children when they are presented intelligently.

These lofty goals might seem impossible for a group of 11 and 12 year olds, but through hard work and empowerment they realized all but one of their goals: that of getting their book published.

The First Generation succeeded in producing a quality newsletter, and parts of it were featured in the quarterly newsletter of the New Hampshire Wildlife Federation. They researched, edited, and entered their product into a word processor, developed a group of subscribers, and helped to pay for the materials.

The book was based on environmental issues which they felt were very important. They followed the same processes as in the newsletter and put together a work that is of high quality. GreenKids also had the opportunity to visit other schools to talk about their experiences and to help others start their own activist groups. Letters were written to persons in power to expand recycling. Their posters and works were featured at town meetings and in the media. But the year was ending and the completed, illustrated book was not published.

GreenKids Second Generation decided to make these goals its yearly objective. Keep the newsletter going, get the school to recycle, buy trees for all nursery school and K-5 students, promote community cleanups, and raise funds to publish the book.

The students supported their GreenKids predecessors by putting out donation cans, having bake sales, and selling newsletters. They won the Proctor & Gamble Scholastic Regional "Waste Not" Award for the recycling project they helped to establish at Lafayette Regional. Through negotiation and hard work they made a contract with a small, local publishing house to produce the book.

All during this time the students continued to research new environmental issues that were important to them. For their efforts the GreenKids I and II won a Presidential Award for Youth Environmental Education. Through letter writing and a media blitz put together by those who wanted to go, the GreenKids raised enough funds to take 15 members of the group to accept the award. All of those who made the deadline and attended after school meetings went to Washington, DC to receive the award.

GreenKids Third Generation continued to write the newsletter, make signs for the tri-town recycling center, conduct a composting project at the school in the spring, recycle milk and juice boxes at school, continue the gardening project, put together an Envirofair in the spring, research for a Peace Corps partner in Senegal, and promote the book, *GreenKids II, A Book for Kids by Kids*.

Media interactions are the responsibility of the students. They have been featured in the *Boston Globe*, New Hampshire Public Radio, *Earth Preservers Magazine*, *National Geographic World*, as well as many local publications. The students interact with reporters and know what their responsibilities are. All GreenKids are given the opportunity to be interviewed and go on exhibitions to other schools to speak. GreenKids Third Generation has just been awarded the Stony Field Farms "Movers and Shakers" Award for Community Volunteerism.

What are GreenKids Fourth Generation doing? This group continues to produce the newsletter, ran a recycled holiday ornament contest at the winter concert, coordinated "Treecycle," a Christmas tree recycling project for the area, started a full scale aluminum recycling project at the school and will be part of the community planting project this spring. All this while attempting to establish a children's environmental theater.

Helping Animals

Since 1988, the fourth and fifth grade students of Columbia Elementary School in Bellingham, Wash. have worked with the Bellingham Whatcom County Humane Society and S.P.C.A. in a project which encourages active citizenship through meaningful student action.

The project is simple in nature, but affords the students an abundance of opportunities to make a difference in the community. Each week a small group of fourth and fifth graders travels out to the Humane Society animal shelter with their teacher. The students are given a tour of the facility and have an opportunity to see first-hand the mission of the Humane Society.

Working with the staff of the shelter, the students select one animal to "interview." Equipped with note sheets and pencils, these young citizens turn into newspaper reporters. They find out important data about the animal which will be related in a news story. The story is sent to the local newspaper, the *Bellingham Herald*, where it is published each Saturday along with a photograph of the animal. All of this work, the trip to the shelter, the writing and editing of the story, and the delivery of the story to the newspaper office is undertaken on a volunteer basis after school hours. This helps instill in these young people the sense of volunteering and shows a commitment to helping the community.

While the newspaper story is the overt product which is shared with the community, the spinoffs from this project are numerous for the students. A group of students and parents helped spruce up the animals' exercise yard by moving and spreading 17 yards of beauty bark. As the director of the shelter said, "Frankly, the spot was an eye-sore before the pruners, shovels, wheelbarrows, and rakes went to work."

Numerous students have written letters to businesses soliciting sites for Humane Society collection banks. A number of student essays have come from this project. Some were used for a student essay page published in the newspaper. Others were written for the 1990 Humane Society essay competition and winners were chosen to be speakers at the Bellingham Whatcom Humane Society awards banquet.

In 1992, the students organized and carried out an animal film festival. Titled "Fifth Graders' Furry Friends Film Festival," the night involved parents, siblings, grandparents and other relatives, and friends. The students turned their lunchroom into a theater complete with tickets and a concession stand. The $113.27 raised was donated for cat identification tags, an item on the Humane Society's "wish list." People attending this event also brought other items needed by the shelter including animal food, blankets, towels, bath mats, and small animal cages. In 1993, another film festival was conducted. The goal was to raise enough money to help the shelter purchase a microscope for daily use. The students raised more than $200.

Several times, the fourth and fifth graders have been invited by Tim Lucy, education director for the Humane Society, to share their experiences and knowledge on his weekly radio show carried on KGMI radio throughout Whatcom County. With the help of a singer/songwriter, students wrote a theme song for the Humane Society. This song was used at a shelter "open house." More than 1,000 community members attended this special event. In 1992, the project was enlarged in scope. With the positive feedback to the managing editor of the *Bellingham Herald* from readers of the "Pets Need People" column, the newspaper agreed to carry the column for the entire school year.

In 1993, several students were afforded the opportunity to visit a board of directors meeting for the Bellingham Whatcom County Humane Society. These students saw the role played by volunteers who serve on the various boards of non-profit agencies in the community.

The young students understand that being good citizens means reaching out and helping others in their community. For their volunteer work, the students won a national merit award through the Kids Can Project sponsored by Scholastic News.

Kids For a Clean Environment

In 1989, Melissa Poe, a fourth grader in Nashville, Tennessee, founded a children's environmental club called Kids For A Clean Environment or Kids F.A.C.E.® In three years the club has grown from a group of six within her elementary school to a positive, proactive international youth organization with more than 200,000 members. She also writes for the newsletter she created for her club which has a worldwide distribution of 2 million.

In August 1989, Melissa began an ongoing campaign to encourage children and adults to become involved with the protection of our natural resources. Kids F.A.C.E. started when Melissa wrote a letter about the environment to the President of the United States. Dissatisfied with the President's initial response, she decided to take action on her own.

In January 1990, she appeared on NBC's "Today" show after writing a letter requesting an appearance. In April of 1990, 250 billboards were placed nationwide with her letter to the President. She also began speaking to encourage children to get involved, and she established chapters of Kids F.A.C.E. In May, 1990, she wrote a letter to Wal-Mart Corp. asking for help for her club, and in November 1990, she created the club newsletter: *Kids F.A.C.E. Illustrated*. Melissa currently writes articles for the newsletter.

In October 1991, she drafted the "Children's Forest" concept with another organization and prepared and circulated petitions. In September 1992, she launched Kids F.A.C.E. "Save-A-Tree" project with tree planting programs (206 trees were planted). In January 1993, she created the design for International Kid's Earth Flag and began the campaign to get kids to help make the flag.

Kids For A Clean Environment is an international children's environmental organization whose purpose is to sponsor educational, community-wide programs in order to further children's involvement in environmental causes; to present information to children concerning the environment and the detrimental effects of pollution and waste on the environment, and to sponsor membership organizations designed to heighten awareness of hazards to the environment and ways of curbing such hazards.

In the accomplishment of these goals, Kids F.A.C.E. will provide free membership packets to youth wishing to form a club or be a club member. Packets will provide detailed steps on formation of the club, member certificates, and suggested projects or activities. The newsletter will be provided on a bi-monthly basis and will also contain suggested projects or activities. Kids F.A.C.E., whenever possible, will work to assist local chapter clubs with environmental resource information, additional support agencies, and local, as well as national, project development.

"Don't think that just because you're a kid that there's nothing you can do. If you are upset about something, or worried about something, then do something! Even if it is just writing a letter, it could be the first step to doing something really big." For more information write to Kids for a Clean Environment (address listed in resource guide).

Operation: Read-Aloud

At the beginning of the 1991-1992 school year, the students of the sixth grade gifted and talented resource class of C.H. Daniels Intermediate School of the Center Independent School District, Center, Texas, were introduced to Community Problem Solving. The students brainstormed for ideas and talked about pollution, crime, drugs, and other topics, but they did not feel that they had touched on the problem that they wished to attack. The next week, a friend brought a book entitled *The New Read-Aloud Handbook,* by Jim Trelease. Presto! As they began to share this book, and think about conditions in their county, they knew without a doubt that they must do something about the lack of interest in reading.

They asked, "How might we, a class of 16 sixth-grade, concerned students, convince parents in the community to take immediate action to improve the lives of their children, and those yet unborn, by reading aloud to, or reading with, their children for at least 15 minutes a day?"

The first activity was to design bookmarks about reading which were printed at a local shop. Little did they know that as they read to children, talked to parents, and distributed the bookmarks at the East Texas Poultry Festival, they were igniting an Operation: Read-Aloud campaign.

One of the facets of Community Problem Solving is involving others. They were pleased that their teacher's daughter, who teaches in a neighboring town, asked for her class to join them in their work. This was the first time in the history of the state contest that two schools had joined together to enter the Community Problem Solving Project. After acquiring these 21 new students, their project spread across into another county. Also involved were fifth grade gifted and talented students who served as a support group and helped them with many of the activities.

The students asked the county judge to declare November 10, 1991, to November 10, 1992, as Operation: Read-Aloud Year. They communicated with local, county, state, and national officials. They contacted religious leaders, school administrators, parent–teachers organizations, county extension agents, and others to tell them of the campaign. They contacted a local radio station and produced radio spots which made the public more aware of the efforts to make the area a better place by promoting reading in the home.

They produced an Operation: Read-Aloud tape, which was based on key ideas from their research. Student-written poems were added. A video entitled, "As the Pages Turn," was produced, which encouraged young people to become authors. The students wrote books for young children. It was a wonderful way to encourage reading and writing.

They spoke to Parents in Public Elementary Education, and appeared on the local program, "Coffee Shop," which is televised by a local church. There were questions that let them express their message of the importance of reading in the home.

They were excited when they received news from a television station that they had won two places in their Public Service Announcement contest. Two of their poems were submitted and adapted for the PSAs. The announcements were aired for several months. When the television crew came to the school, the students worked for about four hours to make two, 30-second announcements. This was an eye-opening experience for them.

They placed posters, banners, and a large mural in the community to proclaim the message. A total of 3,250 letters, along with student designed bookmarks, were sent to the parents of pre-kindergarten through sixth grade students of their school and five other school districts in the county. Parents were asked to sign a pledge to read aloud to or with their children for at least 15 minutes a day. Each student who returned a pledge was eligible for a drawing for book prizes.

The local newspaper was most helpful in printing numerous articles, poems, etc., that were submitted. Also, 72 pastors were asked to mention in their sermons on the first Sunday of 1992, the importance of sharing good literature in the home. One pastor gave the project coverage in an international newsletter that was sent out to 84 countries. One of the poems, "When Mother Reads Aloud," was included in this publication. One of their most rewarding experiences was when the students visited classrooms and read to kindergarten through third grade students.

Operation: Read-Aloud received first place in Community Problem Solving in the State of Texas. This allowed the group to attend the Future Problem Solving Bowl in Austin, Texas. They presented a skit about their project on the stage of the Lyndon Baines Johnson Auditorium and received their award.

As a result of receiving first place in state, the group automatically had an invitation to the International Future Problem Solving Conference in Madison, Wisconsin in June 1992. The group placed sixth at the international conference. Many individuals and groups joined together to raise more than $10,000 that allowed all 16 students and six sponsors to participate in the six-day trip which allowed them to become a part of a whirlwind of activities involving approximately 1,500 students from the United States and several foreign countries.

When International Future Problem Solving began to prepare a videotape for the opening ceremony of the 1993 International Future Problem Solving Conference, they chose one of the group's PSAs to include. This was the only material from the state of Texas that was a part of the video.

Truly, Operation: Read-Aloud had its impact on Shelby County, Texas, as seeds were planted to encourage parents to read aloud to their children for at least 15 minutes a day. It also encouraged the 1992-1993 class to do Community Problem Solving with Patriotism Plus which won third place in Texas. The 1993-1994 group formed the EnviroKids group which has won first place in Texas. If one class leads as Operation: Read-Aloud did, others will follow and a chain of young people taking leadership positions will help to make the world a better place.

S.O.S.

Growing up in Saratoga Springs, NY, Bill Burke-White noticed that some people saw young teenagers as liabilities rather than assets to the community. He wanted to change this perception and demonstrate that teenagers can make a major contribution. Bill believed that his peers would want to be involved in making the world a better place if they were given the opportunity to serve. He also noted a very real need for volunteers in many charitable organizations throughout the community. Putting these observations together, he decided to create a student-based volunteerism club called Student Organized Sharing (S.O.S.). The mission of S.O.S. was established as follows: "To unite concerned students with identified community needs and to provide an opportunity for junior and senior high school students to share their time, energy, and skills for the betterment of our local and global community."

Bill chose the name S.O.S. for the organization since these three letters represent the essence of the club. S.O.S. is the international distress signal calling for help for one's ship. The symbol of the organization is the Morse Code, three dots, three dashes and three dots, that expresses the distressed situation and the call for help. He felt that our planet needed help, starting at the level of the individual and the local community and leading to the global issues and solutions. The acronym "S.O.S." was thus chosen to represent both the new organization's purpose—to bring help to Earth, and the source of its energy—student organized sharing.

To create S.O.S., he met with community leaders and representatives of charitable organizations to identify needs that might be met through student volunteerism. Several months of brainstorming, meetings, and letter writing led to a list of community organizations that were interested in student help.

Bill then compiled a computerized data bank which listed descriptions of these volunteer opportunities. The data bank identified the coordinating charitable organizations, the types of needs, the hours, the sought-after skills, the contact person, and an address and telephone number.

Once he had determined the community's needs, he met with school officials to gain approval for a school-based volunteerism group. Bill then distributed flyers and posters to students in the junior and senior high schools and also to members of local youth organizations such as the Girl Scouts, the Boy Scouts, the 4-H, etc. These materials explained the concept of sharing and volunteerism and encouraged students to participate in these activities. While raising the awareness about identified community needs, these brochures described how much the students themselves could gain from the hours that they might donate.

On an on-going basis, Bill contacted all participating charitable and service organizations and attempted to identify tasks that might be performed by student volunteers, such as reading to the blind, visiting with the elderly at nursing homes, collecting food and used clothing, escorting the handicapped to a parade or a community event, helping in the food pantry, assisting in environmental and restoration projects, tutoring "at risk" elementary and preschool children, doing a handicapped access survey of the downtown, working at the animal shelter, and assisting in the public library. Where necessary, Bill helped these organizations identify new tasks that would be uniquely appropriate for a younger volunteer to make a meaningful contribution.

When he held his first after school organizational meeting, Bill was overwhelmed by a standing-room-only crowd of students eager to get volunteer assignments. The response to the first flyer certainly proved that teenagers are not an apathetic generation! Each of the interested students filled out a data card with his or her name, phone number, interests, skills, experience, available times, transportation needs, etc. Bill entered this information in his computer, paralleling the data on the organizations. Regular meetings were held to link volunteers with organizations. Once volunteers selected their organizations, he accompanied them to their first volunteer sessions and acquainted them with the selected organization.

Bill kept the community aware of the progress of S.O.S. through local newspaper announcements of the after school meetings and human interest stories of various volunteerism activities. As a result of such coverage and awareness, new needs and new service ideas were generated. As the community learned about the work S.O.S. was doing, many people developed a new respect for teenagers and realized that many teens are eager to help their communities and their world.

Though Bill moved with his family to another part of the country, he is really proud to say that S.O.S. is still serving the Saratoga community now, almost four years since it was founded. He feels that this is real evidence of creating a shared vision among the student volunteers. His successor as head of S.O.S. and all the volunteers felt they had ownership of the idea. In fact, S.O.S. has expanded from it's original 50 volunteers to more than 100 who give their time to more than 15 community organizations. The club is still completely student coordinated with limited adult involvement. Every year S.O.S. grows to serve more people and improve the community to an ever greater extent. In four years, volunteers have given thousands of hours to help the elderly in nursing homes, to restore historic sites, to help child care programs, and to deliver food to less fortunate members of the community.

S.O.S. has really made a difference in Saratoga Springs. Everyone has benefitted as volunteerism has become part of the daily lives of the teenage members of the community, developing future concerned and caring citizens, raising everyone's awareness of current community problems, and helping to seek and create solutions. Junior and senior high school students learned to use and to value their time and discovered that a small gesture can make a very big difference. The students also continue to learn new skills and to develop confidence in the skills that they have as their efforts are recognized and appreciated. The work of S.O.S. has resulted in community-wide appreciation for the young volunteers and has given the teenagers a sense of belonging and meaning.

Bill Burke-White, 17, who will enter Harvard in Fall 1994, was selected as one of the top 20 high school students in the country as a member of *USA Today's* 1994 All American Academic Team. Bill received a Westinghouse Science Finalist Scholarship and placed as first runner up to the top 10 Westinghouse Scholars. Fluent in Russian, Bill conducted his primary Westinghouse research at Moscow State University's Institute of Protein Research in Puschino, Russia, where he developed a conceptual model for the control of a genetic mechanism which can change and mutate gene expression. Bill's research has contributed to the further understanding of carcinogenesis and genetic diseases.

An Eagle Scout, Bill has been nationally recognized as a "Creative Altruist" for founding and leading student volunteerism programs in New York and New Hampshire. For the past four years, Bill was a scholarship student at Phillips Exeter Academy, where he served as a director of ESSO, Exeter's Student Service Organization, and as the head of Hospice student volunteers. Bill was also the manager of WPEA-FM, which recently won the Marconi Award as America's "Most Outstanding High School Radio Station." As news manager for the radio station Bill created innovative public service and interview programming.

In 1992, Bill won an Earthwatch Fellowship to conduct paleontological research at a dinosaur excavation in Montana. Bill has also participated in Outward Bound, and for three summers he has studied with the Johns Hopkins University Center for Talented Youth (CTY).

An accomplished elocutionist, Bill was a finalist in New York State's Martin Luther King Arts and Science Elocution Contest for four consecutive years and, as the first place winner in 1990, was the guest speaker with Gov. Mario Cuomo for New York State's Martin Luther King Day ceremonies. In 1990, Bill was also named the Outstanding Youth in the State of New York by the International Juvenile Officers' Association and was the recipient of a New York State Legislative Resolution recognizing his contribution to the memory and awareness of King's words and dreams.

Bill maintains a highest honors average, plays on the Exeter varsity squash team, loves downhill skiing, and is learning to be a bagpiper. Raised in a single parent/single child household, Bill experienced a supplemental cultural awareness curriculum created for him by his mother. Together, over the past 10 years, they have studied the archaeology, mythology, art, history, and literature of ancient and contemporary cultures and have then traveled to, lived, and/or studied in diverse countries from Greece and Turkey to China and Tibet, from England and Scotland to Italy and Paris, Mexico and Peru. In addition Bill has lived and researched in both the then Soviet Union (1990) and in Russia (1993, 1994). Bill considers himself a global citizen and expresses a commitment to the pursuit of a non- violent, ecologically sustainable global community.

Saving a Baby

A student in sixth grade in the Mark Twain Elementary School in Miamisburg, Ohio, approached his teacher and showed the newspaper article that appeared in the *Dayton Daily News* on October 15, 1991. That morning in class, the teacher read the article and all agreed that they could help Carissen Finzel, a six-month-old baby in need of a bone marrow transplant, an experimental procedure not normally covered by insurance. The family had already lost its older twin daughters to a similar disease. The students were not old enough to give blood, so they suggested that they raise money to help pay for bone marrow typing. This would take some of the financial burden from the family. Thus, their community project began. The students became familiar with bone marrow transplants and the national need for other types of transplants. With this need in mind, the students were ready to begin their project to help baby Carissen.

They contacted the management at Kroger Grocery Store to get approval to sell candy bars in front of the store. Receiving an "OK" for selling, the students proceeded in making banners to publicize the sale.

Then on October 16, 1991, eleven days after the public announcement of Carissen's transplant, the students and parents of students sold candy bars. They began at 9 a.m. and were sold out by 1 p.m. The group sold 532 candy bars. At a dollar each, the group made $532.

A big reason for the success was the willingness for other stores next to Kroger to let them also sell candy bars in front of their stores. The managers of the other stores saw what they were doing and allowed them to ask patrons of their store to buy the candy bars to help Carissen.

The class contacted the public relations director at the Dayton Mall and explained the goal to her. She was overjoyed in being a part of their project. The students were allowed to use the gazebo in the center of the mall to sell candy bars.

On November 7, 14, 21, and December 12 and 13 the students again volunteered to sell candy bars to help Carissen. Twenty-six students from the sixth grade developmentally handicapped class, and eight parent chaperones joined the effort. They worked from 5-9 p.m. on each of these nights. In a total of five nights, working just 20 hours, the students raised a total of $2,300.

The goal of selling candy bars at the Dayton Mall was very effective. Not only did the students make a lot of money to donate to Carissen Finzel and the National Marrow Donor Program, they saw in action people helping people—a valuable lesson that only community involvement can teach.

The money was contributed to the Carissen Finzel Bone Marrow Fund and was used for donor blood testing to find a match for her. Carissen received a bone marrow transplant in April 1993.

The students have received the Kids Care Award from Scholastic News for their community volunteerism. They have also been recognized by the National Marrow Donation Program.

Although Carissen lost her battle with the disease and died in April 1993, the students from Mark Twain Elementary remain proud. Their efforts gave Carissen hope, and the donors who joined the marrow registry continue to give hope to other patients like Carissen. The students involved in this project have provided an example of caring for and responding to the needs of others.

Leadership Action
Journal

Chapter 1 Journal Entries
Defining Leadership

Chapter 1
Defining Leadership

My definition of leadership is _____

_____

_____

_____

_____

_____

My friends' definitions of leadership are _____

_____

_____

_____

_____

_____

My definition of leadership for the 21st century is _____

_____

_____

_____

_____

_____

Design a bumper sticker which will tell what you think leadership is.

The color of leadership is _____

_____

_____

The smell of leadership is _____

_____

_____

The taste of leadership is _____

_____

_____

The touch of leadership is _____

_____

_____

The sound of leadership is _____

_____

_____

How is leadership connected to each of the parts of the web?

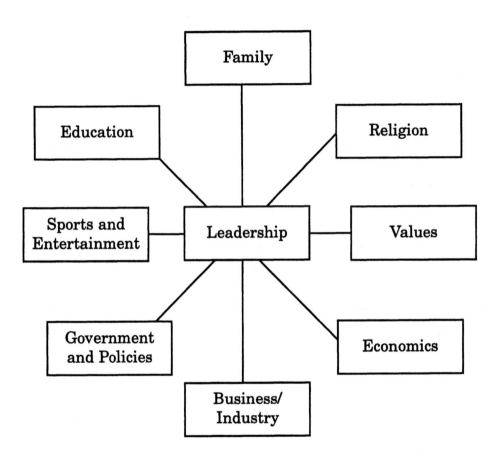

List the characteristics of leadership and rate yourself.
1 = I have; 2 = I need to improve; 3 = I need to develop

Characteristics   Self Rating

_____   _____

_____   _____

_____   _____

_____   _____

_____   _____

_____   _____

_____   _____

_____   _____

_____   _____

_____   _____

_____   _____

_____   _____

_____   _____

_____   _____

Characteristics of leadership that people are born with

Characteristics of leadership that people must learn

List some positive aspects of leadership.

_____

_____

_____

_____

_____

_____

_____

_____

_____

_____

_____

_____

_____

_____

_____

_____

Changes in Leadership Over Time

Tribal Leadership _____

_____

_____

Leadership in Royalty _____

_____

_____

Democratic Leadership _____

_____

_____

Cooperative or Shared Leadership _____

_____

_____

Positive Aspects of Leadership in Today's Society _____

_____

_____

Design a poster of leaders and what each would say are the positive aspects of leadership.

What are the negative aspects of leadership?

Not all aspects of leadership are positive. List what you consider to be the negative aspects of leadership and how you can turn them into positives.

Negatives ➤ Positives

_____   _____

_____   _____

_____   _____

_____   _____

_____   _____

_____   _____

_____   _____

_____   _____

_____   _____

_____   _____

_____   _____

_____   _____

_____   _____

_____   _____

Chapter 2 Journal Entries
Assessing Yourself as a Leader

Sample Campaign Speech Outline

I want to run for this office because _____

_____

_____

My strengths are _____

_____

_____

My goals for this office are _____

_____

_____

You should vote for me because _____

_____

_____

Set goals that are possible. Only promise what you can do. Remember to be creative in how you deliver your thoughts. Humor works well, but don't overdo it!

Ways I have been a leader in school:	Ways I have been a leader in the community:	Ways I have been a leader in my religious affiliation:
_____	_____	_____
_____	_____	_____
_____	_____	_____
_____	_____	_____
_____	_____	_____
_____	_____	_____
_____	_____	_____
_____	_____	_____
_____	_____	_____

Circle the leadership roles you have enjoyed the most.

The reasons why I liked the roles I circled are _____

_____

_____

The reasons why I didn't like the non-circled roles are _____

_____

_____

Extracurricular activities in which I would like to be involved and strategies for doing so are:

Activities	**Strategies**

Plan for a "Leader of the Month" program

- What is the purpose of the proposed program?

- How will you promote it?

- Who will you need to help you get it started?

- What qualifications will be required to be recognized as "Leader of the Month?"

- How will the recipients be selected?

- How will the recipients be recognized?

- What local businesses or groups will help support this program?

- What are other ways you can promote and advertise the program?

- What creative ways can you come up with for getting other young people excited about the program?

Strong Areas of Leadership Skill

List your strengths in leadership skills.

_____   _____

_____   _____

_____   _____

Put those same strengths in order of strongest to least strong.

_____

_____

_____

_____

_____

_____

Select a leader you admire and list his or her strengths in the area of leadership.

_____   _____

_____   _____

_____   _____

How do they compare to yours?

Leadership Analogies

A leader is like a *(animal)* because _____

_____

_____

_____

A leader is like a *(inanimate object)* because _____

_____

_____

_____

A leader is like a *(plant)* because _____

_____

_____

_____

A leader is like a *(shape)* because _____

_____

_____

_____

Weak Areas of Leadership Skill

Weaknesses   **Strategies for Improvement**

Ask an adult who is close to you to discuss these ideas with you.

Chapter 3 Journal Entries
Opportunities for Leadership

Opportunities for Leadership in the School

Complete the following statements.

I would like to have the following opportunities for leadership in my school _____

_____

_____

_____

_____

_____

_____

I plan to develop more opportunities for leadership in my school by

_____

_____

_____

_____

_____

_____

_____

Leadership Positions in My School

List all of the scholastic and sports leadership positions in your school. Circle the ones that are the most important to you.

Scholastic Responsibilities	Sports Responsibilities
_____	_____
_____	_____
_____	_____
_____	_____
_____	_____
_____	_____
_____	_____
_____	_____
_____	_____
_____	_____
_____	_____

Develop a plan to lead one or more of the above.

Elected positions of leadership in the school	Ways that a person can be a leader in school without being elected to office
_____	_____
_____	_____
_____	_____
_____	_____
_____	_____
_____	_____
_____	_____
_____	_____
_____	_____
_____	_____
_____	_____
_____	_____
_____	_____
_____	_____
_____	_____

Opportunities for Leadership in My Community

Complete the following statement.

I want to be a leader in my community because _____

_____

_____

_____

_____

_____

_____

_____

_____

_____

_____

_____

_____

_____

Make a list of things that you would like to begin or change in your community.

Begin   Change

_____   _____

_____   _____

_____   _____

_____   _____

_____   _____

_____   _____

_____   _____

_____   _____

_____   _____

_____   _____

_____   _____

_____   _____

_____   _____

Make a plan to lead in one or more of these areas.

Community Leaders as Mentors

Mentor	Area of Interest
Name _____	
Address _____	
_____	
Phone _____	

Mentor	Area of Interest
Name _____	
Address _____	
_____	
Phone _____	

Mentor	Area of Interest
Name _____	
Address _____	
_____	
Phone _____	

Mentor	Area of Interest
Name _____	
Address _____	
_____	
Phone _____	

Contact these potential mentors and ask for a time when they can meet with you and you can observe them in their leadership activities.

Opportunities for Leadership in My Church, Temple, or Religious Affiliation

Make a list of leadership activities you would like available in your religious affiliation.

_____	_____
_____	_____
_____	_____
_____	_____
_____	_____
_____	_____
_____	_____
_____	_____
_____	_____
_____	_____
_____	_____

Circle the one you think is the most important.
Write and carry out a plan for getting the activity started.

Elected positions of leadership for young people in your religious affiliation

Ways that a young person can be a leader without being elected to office

_____

_____

_____

_____

_____

_____

_____

_____

_____

_____

_____

_____

_____

_____

_____

_____

_____

_____

_____

_____

_____

_____

_____

_____

_____

_____

_____

_____

_____

_____

Chapter 4 Journal Entries
Training for Leadership

School file of resource people for leadership training:

Person

Name _____

Address _____

_____

Phone _____

Area of Leadership Training

Person

Name _____

Address _____

_____

Phone _____

Area of Leadership Training

Person

Name _____

Address _____

_____

Phone _____

Area of Leadership Training

Person

Name _____

Address _____

_____

Phone _____

Area of Leadership Training

What opportunities do you have for training in your community?

Community File of Leadership
Programs for Youth

Program	Contact Information	Type of Program
_____	Name: _____	_____
_____	Address: _____	_____
_____	_____	_____
_____	Name: _____	_____
_____	Address: _____	_____
_____	_____	_____
_____	Name: _____	_____
_____	Address: _____	_____
_____	_____	_____
_____	Name: _____	_____
_____	Address: _____	_____
_____	_____	_____
_____	Name: _____	_____
_____	Address: _____	_____
_____	_____	_____

Community leadership training programs that I have attended:

Program:	Positive Points:	Negative Points:
_____	_____	_____
_____	_____	_____
_____	_____	_____
_____	_____	_____
_____	_____	_____
_____	_____	_____
_____	_____	_____
_____	_____	_____
_____	_____	_____
_____	_____	_____
_____	_____	_____
_____	_____	_____
_____	_____	_____
_____	_____	_____

Develop a handbook of the ones that you would recommend.

Chapter 5 Journal Entries
Influence and Encouragement from Others

Parental Influences on Leadership

My current responsibilities at home:

_____

_____

_____

_____

_____

_____

_____

Responsibilities I would like to have at home: _____

_____

_____

_____

_____

_____

Talk with your parents about these responsibilities and set up a plan for getting started.

I. Persons who have already
    influenced me to be a
    leader:

How they have influenced
leadership abilities:

_____

_____

_____

_____

_____

II. Persons who could have
    an influence on my leader-
    ship abilities in the
    future:

How they could be of help
to me as I develop leadership skills:

_____

_____

_____

_____

_____

Contact the persons listed in Part I to thank them.
Contact the persons listed in Part II to ask for their help.

Encouraging your Child of the Future

Dear Child:

My hopes for you as a leader are _____

_____

_____

I will try to be a good leader and role model for you by _____

_____

_____

It is important to me that you learn to make decisions because

_____

_____

Other ways I plan to help you develop as a leader are _____

_____

_____

If you feel comfortable with your responses, share these with your parents. It may help them learn of other ways they can encourage you as a leader.

Teachers' Influence

Teachers can have a very positive influence on their students' leadership ability by _____

_____

_____

Sometimes teachers discourage leadership in their students by

_____

_____

Sometimes school elections are based on popularity rather than leadership. Teachers could help discourage this by _____

_____

_____

Leadership is an important area to be developed in the youth of today because _____

_____

_____

Write your responses to these and other statements about leadership in an editorial. Get other responses from students of all races, gender, and socioeconomic levels. Share these with your principal and teachers.

Chapter 6 Journal Entries
Great Leaders

Nomination Form
Leaders' Hall of Fame

I nominate _____

This person was (is) a great leader because _____

_____

_____

_____

_____

_____

_____

People will always remember this person for the accomplishment of

_____

_____

_____

_____

_____

_____

_____

Riddles and Puzzles about Great Leaders

Riddles _____

_____

_____

_____

_____

_____

_____

Puzzles _____

_____

_____

_____

_____

_____

_____

_____

Styles of Leadership

Great autocratic leaders

_____

_____

_____

_____

Great *laissez faire* leaders

_____

_____

_____

_____

Great democratic leaders

_____

_____

_____

_____

Past Leaders on Current Issues

Past Leaders   Current Issues

_____   _____

_____   _____

_____   _____

_____   _____

_____   _____

_____   _____

_____   _____

_____   _____

_____   _____

_____   _____

_____   _____

_____   _____

Match any past leader to a current issue and discuss how you think
he or she may have responded to it.

Great Leaders Matrix

International	National	State	Community/Regional	
				Education
				Government
				Humanities
				Mathematics
				Medicine
				Politics
				Religion
				Science/Technology
				Sports
				Performing Arts
				Business/Industry

Chapter 7 Journal Entries
Advice to Others

Leadership positions that I would like
to have in the future

School Position   Year

_____ _____

_____ _____

_____ _____

_____ _____

_____ _____

Community Position   Year

_____ _____

_____ _____

_____ _____

_____ _____

_____ _____

Religious Position   Year

_____ _____

_____ _____

_____ _____

_____ _____

Choose five great leaders and develop a skit based on the advice each would give.

Great Leaders   Advice

_____   _____

_____   _____

_____   _____

_____   _____

_____   _____

_____   _____

_____   _____

_____   _____

_____   _____

_____   _____

_____   _____

_____   _____

Be sure to use these for a skit. You'll need stage props, costumes, and students for roles. Don't forget to get an audience.

Television Commercial Script

In 30 seconds, encourage younger students to become leaders.

Words   Pictures

_____   _____

_____   _____

_____   _____

_____   _____

_____   _____

_____   _____

_____   _____

_____   _____

_____   _____

_____   _____

_____   _____

_____   _____

Take or send this to your local television station.

Leadership Action Forms

Letter to Obtain More Information

Date

Mr., Mrs., or Ms., Janet/Joe Leadership
100 Leadership Drive
Leader, Leadership 00000

Dear (Ms., Mrs., or Mr.) Leadership:

I am very interested in getting involved with your organization and would like more information. Please send me any brochures, pamphlets, or other materials on your organization and any other resources that may be available relating to ___(topic)___.

I appreciate your attention to my request, and I look forward to getting involved with _(name of organization)_!

Sincerely,

(Name)

Contact Log

Person, Title, Address, Telephone number	Reason	Result
_____	_____	_____
_____	_____	_____
_____	_____	_____
_____	_____	_____
_____	_____	_____
_____	_____	_____
_____	_____	_____
_____	_____	_____
_____	_____	_____
_____	_____	_____
_____	_____	_____
_____	_____	_____
_____	_____	_____
_____	_____	_____
_____	_____	_____

Interviews

Purpose: _____

_____

_____

Person Interviewed: _____   Title: _____

Organization: _____

Address: _____

_____

Date: _____   Time: _____

| Questions | | Responses |

Interviewer _____
School/Club _____

Thank You Letter

Mr., Mrs., or Ms. Janet/Joe Leadership
100 Leadership Drive
Leader, Leadership 00000

Dear (Mr., Mrs., or Ms.) Leadership:

Thank you for your help with _____. We appreciate your time and effort. Your assistance will always be remembered.

Sincerely,

(Name)

Leadership Development Plan

My goal   _____

_____

_____

Objectives   _____

_____

_____

Resources/
People   _____

_____

_____

Other   _____

_____

_____

Timeline   _____

_____

_____

Surveys

A survey may take many forms with several response modes. Two examples are: yes or no; and strongly agree (SA), undecided (U), don't know (DK).

Caution: Open-ended responses are difficult to tally and most people are more likely to complete a survey if they are not required to write a response. Checking a response is easier.

Question	Response
_____	_____
_____	_____
_____	_____
_____	_____
_____	_____
_____	_____
_____	_____
_____	_____
_____	_____
_____	_____

Tallying Results

	SA	A	D	U	DK		Yes	No
Question						or		

Results and Conclusions: ————————————————————

————————————————————————————————————

————————————————————————————————————

————————————————————————————————————

————————————————————————————————————

————————————————————————————————————

————————————————————————————————————

————————————————————————————————————

————————————————————————————————————

————————————————————————————————————

————————————————————————————————————

Petition Form

Title: _____

_____

_____

Group or Association: _____

Purpose: _____

_____

_____

We would like to initiate or change the following: _____

_____

_____

We agree to the above:

Name	Address	Phone	Date
1. _____ _____	_____	_____
_____		
_____		
2. _____ _____	_____	_____
_____		
_____		

Be sure to check about the number of signatures required.

News Release
For Immediate Release

_____

_____

_____

_____

_____

_____

_____

_____

❏ Newspaper   Name of Contact Person: _____

❏ TV   Address: _____

❏ Radio   _____

A news release should be concisely written and contain only the facts of the story. Be sure to be accurate in facts and names. Like other stories, a news release should give the details including who, what, where, when, why, and conclusions.

Resources

Anchor Clubs
Pilot International Building
P.O. Box 4844
Macon, GA 31213-0599

A service organization for high schoolers. Students participate in community service projects and promote public awareness of brain disorders.

Amnesty International Youth Program
1118 22nd Street, NW
Washington, DC 20037

Local groups of students receive information about human rights abuses worldwide. Students write letters and sponsor community activities to boost awareness of human rights abuses such as torture and political killings.

Boy Scouts of America
P.O. Box 132079
Irving, TX 75015-2079

Boy Scouts is a national network of clubs, devoted to developing the character, leadership, citizenship, and fitness of young men through the age of 18.

Boys and Girls Brigades of America
P.O. Box 9863
Baltimore, MD 21284

A Christian organization for youth aged 6-18. Programs seek to encourage youth leadership skills through outdoor activities, camping, athletics, missions training, and related activities.

Boys and Girls Clubs of America
1230 W. Peachtree Street, N.W.
Atlanta, GA 30309

This youth service organization's primary focus is on youth development. Programs and services are available for youth aged 6-18.

Camp Fire Boys and Girls
4601 Madison Avenue
Kansas City, MO 64112-1278

Camp Fire views itself as "an organization with and of youth, not just for youth." With programs for children of all ages, Camp Fire has a range of opportunities for self-discovery, decision-making, and leadership.

Center for Creative Leadership
P.O. Box 26300
Greensboro, NC 27438-6300

This educational institute offers practical, research-based tools for developing creative leadership potential. Many participants in programs come from business and industry, education, government, and public service backgrounds.

C.L.A.S.S. Program
International Training in Communication
2519 Woodland Drive
Anaheim, CA 92801

The C.L.A.S.S. Program, which stands for Communication, Leadership, and Speaking Skills, is an eight week leadership training program for junior and senior high school students.

Cooperative Extension Service
4-H Youth Development
U.S. Department of Agriculture
Washington, DC 20250

A national program for youth aged 9-19. Local activities vary, but the general emphasis is on leadership development, competition, public speaking, and awareness of natural resources.

Excel Clubs
National Exchange Club
3050 Central Avenue
Toledo, OH 43606-1700

Excel Clubs are high school community service clubs which are dedicated to responsible citizenship and service.

Future Business Leaders of America
1912 Association Drive
Reston, VA 22091

FBLA is an organization for high school and college students who are planning business careers. Chapters are generally run as school clubs.

Future Problem Solving Program
318 W. Ann Street
Ann Arbor, MI 48104

This is a program for students of all ages who are involved in gifted and talented programs. Teams of students from all over the world compete in problem-solving contests that address issues of the future.

Gavel Club
Toastmasters International
P.O. Box 9052
Mission Viejo, CA 92690-7052

Sponsored by Toastmasters International the adult organization devoted to better public speaking, Gavel Club offers opportunities for students to study and participate in speech-making and quality public speaking.

Girl Scouts of the USA
420 Fifth Avenue
New York, NY 10018-2702

Through Girl Scouting programs, girls aged 5-17 learn about personal development, decision-making, life skills, community spirit, and leadership. Activities range from local meetings, to camps, to international conferences.

Hugh O'Brian Youth Foundation
10880 Wilshire Boulevard, Suite 103
Los Angeles, CA 90024

High school sophomores who are nominated by their schools may attend local, regional, and national seminars on leadership.

Inroads St. Louis, Inc.
1221 Locust Street, Suite 800
St. Louis, MO 63103

Inroads trains and places minority youth in business opportunities. Its mission is "to develop and place talented minority youth in business and industry and prepare them for corporate and community leadership."

Interact
Rotary International
1560 Sherman Avenue
1 Rotary Center
Evanston, IL 60201

Sponsored by local rotary clubs, the high school level Interact Clubs are devoted to service, personal responsibility, and integrity, and to the development of leadership skills.

Junior Civitan
Civitan International
P.O. Box 130744
Birmingham, AL 35213-0744

Junior Civitan is a community service club for junior and senior high school students. The clubs usually concentrate on helping persons who are disabled and raising funds to support this cause.

Junior Optimist Octagon International
Optimist International
4494 Lindell Boulevard
St. Louis, MO 63108

Clubs at all grade levels encourage youth involvement in the community. The organization is dedicated to self-improvement through service to the community and awareness of civic affairs.

Junior Statesmen of America
650 Bair Island Road, Suite 201
Redwood City, CA 94063

Junior Statesmen of America is a student-run organization with chapters nationwide. It fosters direct student involvement in the processes of government through numerous debates, mock-government programs, and other activities.

Key Club International
Kiwanis International
3636 Woodview Trace
Indianapolis, IN 46268

A service organization for high school students that is run as a student club. It is the world's largest high school service organization.

Kids for a Clean Environment
P.O. Box 158254
Nashville, TN 37215

Individual members and groups of Kids F.A.C.E. create environmental programs within their own communities and keep in touch with other student activists nationwide. Membership is open to people ages 9 and up. (See story on page 107.)

Leo Club Program
Lions Club International
300 22nd Street
Oakbrook, IL 60521-8842

Leo Clubs, sponsored by local Lions Clubs, are devoted to leadership and service. The clubs are open to girls and boys aged 12-28.

National Association of Student Councils
National Association of Secondary School Principals
1904 Association Drive
Reston, VA 22091

This is an organization to promote student governments, improve communication between students and teachers, and give guidance for student government programs.

National Network of Youth Advisory Boards

P.O. Box 402036
Ocean View Branch
Miami Beach, FL 33140

If your community does not have a student advisory board as part of the local government, this organization can help you get one started. Include a SASE with your request for information.

National Youth Leadership Council, Inc.

1910 W. County Road B
Roseville, MN 55113

NYLC has a variety of programs and publications to help individuals and groups of young people in developing leadership skills.

Odyssey of the Mind

OM Association
P.O. Box 547
Glassboro, NJ 08028

An educational program that encourages the development of creative thinking and problem-solving skills for students kindergarten through high school.

Outward Bound USA

National Headquarters
Route 9D
R2 Box 280
Garrison, NY 10524-9757

Outward Bound wilderness adventure trips provide an opportunity for personal growth in leadership ability and self-esteem. Trips are available in various locations and involve different types of outdoor activity.

Project Service Leadership
12703 NW 20th Avenue
Vancouver, WA 98685

This organization helps schools and communities establish service learning in the schools at all levels.

Serteen
Sertoma International
1912 E. Meyer Boulevard
Kansas City, MO 64132

Serteen is a service organization for high school youth. Clubs raise funds for specific needs in their communities and do service projects to benefit their communities as well.

YMCA Teen Leadership Programs
YMCA of the USA Program Services
101 N. Wacker Drive
Chicago, IL 60606

A program for high school students. Based on the idea that each generation must have a direct understanding of democracy, the program uses model government activities and debate opportunities to develop leadership skills in young people.

Youth for Understanding (YFU) International Exchange
3501 Newark Street, NW
Washington, DC 20016

YFU is a private, non-profit organization dedicated to international understanding and world peace through its cultural exchange program. It offers year, semester, and summer exchange opportunities for high school students.

Get in Touch!

We would like to know your reactions to the ideas and actions presented in this book, therefore, we encourage you to write to us with your comments. Please complete the following form and mail it to us after having completed the book.

Leadership for Students: A Practical Guide
Frances A. Karnes and Suzanne M. Bean

I am a:
❏ student   ❏ teacher   ❏ librarian   ❏ parent
❏ school administrator   ❏ guidance counselor
❏ community leader   ❏ religious leader   ❏ other _____

1. What were your favorite activities in the book?

2. What other leadership related activities have you participated in as a result of reading this book?

3. Who have you helped to get involved in youth leadership development?
❏ friends   ❏ school personnel   ❏ parents
❏ community leader   ❏ religious leader   ❏ other _____

4. Other comments

Mail this form to: Dr. Frances A. Karnes
                            Box 8207
                            University of Southern Mississippi
                            Hattiesburg, MS 39406-8207